NATURE
NURTURE
NEITHER

I0156875

NATURE
NURTURE
NEITHER

A *Family's* JOURNEY
IN *Creativity*

JAN SEALE

Angelina River Press
Fort Worth, Texas

© 2014 Jan Seale
All Rights Reserved

ISBN 978-0-9883844-5-3
Library of Congress Control Number: 2014949620
Manufactured in the United States of America
Cover design by Erren Seale

Angelina River Press, LLC
Fort Worth, Texas

*For all who believe
that the arts
give us our humanity*

CONTENTS

Introduction

A popular pastime these days is writing family stories and that is basically what this book attempts, with a determined emphasis on showing what happened when two people in the arts spawned three children who also became artists. In the coming chapters, without much research or science to back up the assertions, is the autobiography of a family's immersion in the arts.

"Your family is so creative," people often kindly say, and I'm not sure what to reply. "Yes, we are" sounds arrogant. "Not really" is not the truth. I've settled on, "Well, everyone is. It's just that ours is perhaps more public."

What I think they may mean by such a complimentary observation is that we five—two parents and three sons—turned out to be deeply involved in the arts. Other expressions of creative thinking or action—those in the home, the boardroom, or the workplace, may get short shrift, while the arts—ahhh, now *there* is creativity.

Creativity cannot be rationally explained or measured. As a speaker at a creativity seminar lamented, "Trying to pin down creativity is like trying to nail Jell-O to the wall."[1] Yet we all, each one of us, live our daily lives on a layer of universal creativity. Every piece of clothing, kitchen gadget, fixture, communication item, means of transportation, as well as successful theories, research, policies, and plans are the result of the practice of creativity on the part of hordes of creative thinkers forever unknown to us.

Creativity bids us to see things in a new way, to go beyond the information given, recombining, thinking in unconventional ways, using little known or neglected means. To be clinical, it starts in the frontal lobe, "the area in your brain that has the unrelenting capacity to dream up virtually anything."[2]

Still, for the purposes of this book, I accept the equation: creativity=the arts. But only with the foregoing caveat, and with a personal sense of humility and wonderment that the whole of humanity is

1

instilled with the ability and energy to fashion something new, useful, or beautiful.

Of course, the arts contain other elements besides creativity. Among those attributes involving or standing outside creativity are cognitive thinking, patience, application of known materials, historicity, and repeated competencies, that is, skills such as mastering a musical instrument or dancing.

The players on this small family stage include my husband Carl who was for thirty years conductor of the Valley Symphony Orchestra. During this time he also taught at our local university and composed prolifically. In his retirement, he continued to compose and refine his existing compositions. And for several prior years he enjoyed fashioning folk art from various natural plant materials, mainly palm trees.

I have from childhood been a writer of poems and stories. My other passions include teaching creative writing, editing, volunteering on behalf of our local environment, and playing the flute.

Our eldest son Ansen makes his living as a commercial photographer, with an active and ever-growing side of art photography which keeps him busy with projects of public art and showings in galleries in Texas and abroad.

Our middle son Erren trained in commercial art and practiced it very successfully for a number of years before combining that with owning and running a business in cultural items, antiques and home furnishings.

Avrel, the youngest, is a writer and editor, recently moving from the editorship of a university alumni magazine to the position of speech writer for the president of a major university.

(Here I place a little help for you, the reader, about their names. For purposes of this book, I am sorry that the names Ansen and Avrel look so similar. Where I am discussing them individually, I have tried to retain their birth order: listing Ansen the eldest first, then Erren the second-born, then Avrel the youngest. One small mnemonic device: The second letter of "Ansen" (first-born) comes in the alphabet before the second letter of "Avrel" (third-born).)

When asked, "How come you five are like you are?" or some variation of the question, my inclination is to say, "I have no idea." The writer E.M. Forster observed, "How can I tell what I think till I see what I say?"[3] So this book began, to find out the answer to the question.

I had never thought of the question by others as a topic for a book, that is, not until I had an earnest-sounding e-mail from a local young father. "My wife and I would love for our children to embrace the arts for a lifetime and even consider making a career out of a passion they have. What's the secret?"[4] How was it, in our children's upbringing, that they all became artists of some sort?

So what could I say, on the page, to answer this young man? It seemed a worthwhile endeavor to try to elaborate. But the more I thought about it, the more I realized that it wasn't going to be a one-two-three explanation. Why couldn't we say, just to make it simple, that because their father was a musician and their mother a writer, that the boys' destinies were in their genes?

That would have been too simple indeed, but more so, untrue. In David Shenk's words in *The Genius in All of Us,* "Studies have shown that mind-set, nutrition, parenting, peers, media, culture, time, focus, and motivation all profoundly affect the development of abilities."[5]

Yes, nature, but also nurture. Nurture, and that other thing of the title, Neither, designating that elusive element of our sons' own distinct callings and longings and efforts. And one other thing—circumstance, which, though possibly construed as the unplanned part of the environment, remains at least a distinct subset.

But not to totally discount nor give short shrift to the possibilities of inherited genes—of which we will know so much more about in the future with efforts like the Human Genome Project—I have also felt it necessary to give some background on the generations leading up to the present, these hopefully relevant to the subject of our children's bent toward creativity.

In Part Two: Glimpses I have left it to you to catch the drift of daily life of the young family, hoping that by inference one can make some assumptions. Maybe this is a cop-out—a way of putting the burden of proof on the reader. It might also be construed as a game, a sort of multiple choice, where you decide if hours of free play in an old orchard can contribute in a significant way to a child's becoming a photographer, writer, or graphic designer.

Part Three: Presently describes the path each took toward adulthood and his present endeavors.

Part Four: The Home as Lab tries to label some of the aspects of our children's upbringing that we in hindsight feel were important. We did not always know that we were doing these things: they often were the unconscious reactions of our personalities. How they impacted the boys' chosen work is anecdotal at best. Still, sometime the truth may be found in the evidence.

Part Five: Considerations discusses a few personality factors peculiar to our three that possibly shed light on their predilections and work-life choices.

Part Six: Cultivating Creativity offers eight personal precepts on encouraging creativity.

Part Seven: Final Thoughts ends back at the personal. In the appendix, you will find three samples of writing by our sons based on their interests.

If you are looking for a how-to book on raising a creative child, you may not find it here. I've not been able to say with any definiteness just what has made our children turn out as they have. I wouldn't presume to give a formula. But if I did, and with certainty—given my strong upbringing of not bragging about one's achievements—it would seem smug, self-aggrandizing, and obnoxious.

Today the creative Muses remain as elusive as they were when the Greeks identified them. I wrote this book out of curiosity—to see if I could get down in print the path our family took to arrive, somewhat surprised ourselves, at our art-filled destinies.

Despite the randomness of detailed experience, this is not a tell-all book. You will not find juicy controversy or major crises here. Know that we had our spats, our walk-outs and door slammings, our edicts delivered. We had disappointment, tears, and heartaches. We had dismal worry and depression, uncertainty and sorrow, all those trials that every family staying together long enough will experience. Except to mention these in the context of our artistic lives, it seemed specious and belaboring to explore them here.

At times in their upbringing, we parents knew what we were doing—our best selves molding, shaping, and, if truth be known, feeding our own creative monsters by fashioning a creative atmosphere for our children. And then there were the negative flukes of our own life circumstances, such as marrying young, being too much alike, never having enough money—all of which, it seems in part, to have played a role in causing our family to turn out the way it did. Thus, the environment. At other times, we accidentally lived creative lives— stumbling and groping and reveling in the activities we mysteriously enjoyed, products of our heredity.

Some details of this account may seem irrelevant. Some may appear self-serving—a fact that for a long time prevented me from writing. But I forge ahead, with the hope that you will compassionately graze through our history, picking out the parts that may resonate in your own family's life, either presently, in retrospect, or as possibilities in the future. Perhaps you will be content just to be entertained by our bumbling frantic activity, our unscientific way of living out our days, thanks to the arts.

Part One: Beginnings

Music and Poetry Combine

The first day my future husband Carl and I met, we spent the night together. But it was on a bus, in October of 1956, returning overnight from a trip to Fayetteville, Arkansas where the Baylor Bears played the Arkansas Razorbacks. I was a 17-year-old freshman music major, a flute player with a scholarship, and I was highly impressed that he was already 21, a junior music major and the commanding drum major of the Baylor Golden Wave Band.

Just as the sun came up, we pulled onto the campus and I walked to my dorm in a daze, pillow under arm, waking my roommates to tell them about this marvelous handsome guy I had sat with on the bus, how we talked all night, how he had asked me for a date. I don't think I told them that, along toward morning, he had kissed me gently, and I had replied, "I hope you don't think I let every boy do that right off." Okay, it was the fifties; that's the way things were then.

As our courtship galloped forward, I learned that he wanted to be a band director, that he composed music, and that he was from the Rio Grande Valley of Texas—which was somewhere south, right? I had already observed him playing oboe and bassoon in the concert band.

He learned that I was a Baptist preacher's daughter, that I was majoring in music but couldn't figure out what I would do with such a degree, since as a woman, I couldn't be a band or choir director. (Again, it was the fifties.) Maybe I could be a public school music teacher, or a piano teacher...Naw, neither one appealing. All I knew was that I loved playing the flute and piano. Oh, and I liked language too, having written poems since childhood, and I liked to read.

Fast forward: A wedding on Good Friday 1958 in my hometown of Waxahachie, a summer term at Baylor, Carl's graduation at 21 with a Bachelor of Music degree. By this time, the Baylor band had performed one of his compositions. I was an 18-year-old junior, just completing my basic theory and music appreciation classes. That summer, at my flute teacher's urging, I played a solo flute recital. Maybe I *could* be a professional player; still, the whole thing sounded scary. And besides, I was in love. And what if we went to a place where there was only one position in music? Of course, the man would get it.

But another muse was whispering in my ear. For a sophomore English literature course, the prof asked me to play the role of Elizabeth Barrett Browning. I made a surprise appearance to the class dressed in a black taffeta dress and a wig of black shiny curls. On cue, I emerged and intoned two of Browning's sonnets in the most dramatic Victorian voice my central Texas twang could muster. At my appearance, there was a collective gasp from the group, then an awe-struck silence. I was barely eighteen, and I was busy delivering the poet's immortal "How do I love thee?" Something about their reaction went deep into my mind and heart. Look at the power of poetry.

In late August 1958, we loaded up all our worldly possessions and headed to Kentucky and the University of Louisville, where Carl had received a fellowship to be the assistant band director while he got his master's in music. By this time, I had decided to major in English. It was a hot, three-day trip, with no air conditioning. The overhead rack was crammed with luggage. The mop stuck out from one side, the broom from the other. My mother said later that we looked like some giant insect with rear antennae as we pulled away from their house.

We were headed for more music, more literature. What made us compulsively move toward a life in the arts? Even young as we were, we knew there was more money in other vocations. Call it a huge dose of inherited genes.

Ancestral Motifs

Ironically, Carl's father and mother also met in a band. Carl's mother's father, Charles Hewett, was an itinerant orchestra and band leader in the Midwest in the early part of the twentieth century. A virtual Music Man, he moved his family from one small town to another, organizing a musical group and playing concerts until the money ran out and/or he heard of another town wanting someone to head up its music. In the evenings, he directed a vaudeville act dubbed The Musical Hewetts.

In this group Carl's mother played the saxophone, while her siblings played trumpet and violin, and their mother played the piano. They all sang. At first they were one of the main acts but when silent movies were introduced into the theaters, the family was relegated to playing between acts during the changing of the reels.

One day in her sixties, Carl's modest mother observed casually that as a small child, her first attempts at reading were reading words backwards! It seems that the family sat on stage behind the screen during showings as they awaited their turn to entertain the restless audience. Annah's first read words were the subtitles as they filtered through to the back side of the screen.

When Professor Hewett brought his family to Athens, Texas to take a musical position, young Annah, the saxophonist, met a drummer in the band, one Horace Seale. And they were married for fifty years.

Carl had two brothers and a sister. One of those siblings was Larry, Carl's younger brother by ten years, a fine musician who was headed on a music scholarship to Baylor playing bassoon when he died tragically on a senior class outing at South Padre Island in 1963.

Besides music, the graphic arts have also been a part of our children's heritage. Carl's other brother, Harlie, had a long career as a commercial artist and in retirement continued to sculpt and paint. Several cousins made their living as commercial artists as well.

Carl's father was a master artisan in woodworking. He fashioned beautiful furniture, toys, candlesticks, plates, and bowls. And if he found he had no tool for a certain job, he stopped and made the tool.

More genetic strains of showmanship were evident in Carl's cousins, The Flying Beehees of the Barnum and Bailey Circus. This troupe came to Ft. Worth often and Carl's family would visit them behind the Big Top in their quarters. Carl's flair for writing for the stage, in the operas, ballets, and various stage pieces he has done, may have had its beginnings when he as a small boy was taken to ogle the glamorous life of the high-wire performers.

What was passed down to me in music and literature? My maternal grandfather, Charles Pittman, played self-taught hymns and rags on the piano and sang revivals in southeastern Oklahoma. When I was twelve years old, he loaned my parents the $500 needed to buy me a fine sterling silver Haynes flute, which I still play today.

My mother, Margaret, loved music and played the piano and organ throughout her life. She made sure that my sister and I had piano lessons as girls. It didn't hurt that these were free—one of the perks of being the Baptist preacher's daughters.

And the writing? My father's father was an Arkansas preacher-farmer who doted on books. I have some in which his handwriting in the front proclaims, "Worth every penny I paid for this" with a marked price of 75 cents. This grandfather wrote poetry with a serious didactic tone, often in his war on liquor or Catholicism, except when he occasionally broke out into humorous doggerel. He quoted poetry and made scrapbooks of poems cut from newspapers.

Two sons—one of them my father, Thomas Hollis Epton—became Baptist ministers. My father wrote poems frequently and most sermons contained a quoted poem from another source. He also quoted poems at the supper table and often read them to my mother as she labored in the kitchen. In his later years, he became a beloved columnist for the *Waxahachie Daily Light*, writing over 400 weekly columns for his old friends in the small town.

As in my Arkansas grandfather's house, in the parsonage we always had a room devoted to books. I liked to sneak into Dad's study when he was away and pull out a certain volume titled *I Was in Hell with Niemöller*. I was not exactly sure why the author was in hell with Niemöller (a German anti-Nazi theologian), but I remember that particular book, of all his hundreds. It may be that I felt the daring of pronouncing the word "hell" aloud, without any possibility of censure, or it could have been that I was vaguely aware it had to do with Christians imprisoned by the Nazis. Maybe I was intoxicated with the umlauted "o." At any rate, it was a book and it had magic. The apple was not to fall far from the tree.

So here Carl and I were, coming from our musical, artful, and bookish families, grateful to find each other's starry-eyed selves. Did we consider that being an artist was so thoroughly potent and impoverishing that it might be best if one partner in a marriage was more suited to business or science? No, we did not.

On the other hand, there are certain advantages to being equally yoked as artists. I understood his need to compose music, and with my background in music and my flute and piano playing, I could talk performance, music history, and notation with him. As a mutual creator, he could understand my need to write poems and stories, and with his flair for musical drama, talk plot and dramatic effect with me. We didn't have to do a lot of explaining or apologizing to each other for what we did.

We were content to be alone and to let the other be alone for as long as it took to make an artistic statement. We comforted each other in our downturns—the rejected composition, the ill-performed piece, the silence of a publisher, the absence or crankiness of a muse. And we were cheered uncommonly by the other's success—the accepted composition or book, the well-received performance, the happy crowd at a reading—but most of all, the satisfaction of completing a self-assigned work.

I can't say it was all rosy, this marriage of a writer and a musician. There were times when one of us had to sacrifice a precious visit of the muse to household chores or a scout meeting or simply earning enough money to keep us afloat. But a couple of things helped.

For one, neither of us came from homes where we saw entitlement modeled. All our parents were hardworking, load-bearing people. We had no examples of prima donnas. (Okay, granted, most Baptist preachers consider themselves pretty special.)

And the decision to have a family brought a forced practicality to our existence, unlike artists who have no dependents. It is difficult, if not impossible, to write a great poem at five p.m. when there are three hungry sons in the house.

Carl's artistic recognition came from two areas, his conducting of the Valley Symphony Orchestra for thirty years and local performances of his prolific musical compositions. I have had my share of good fortune in being published widely in Texas, with some national notice as well. So we have had our separate audiences. Somehow, we managed to take turns standing in the wings, cheering the other on.

A Go at Parenting: Ansen

Sometimes we laughingly say that our eldest son Ansen has two bachelor's degrees. One was obtained when he moved across the stage under my black robe in 1960 at the University of Louisville, a two-month fetus. The other occurred in the spring of 1982 when he received his B.A. in Communications and Studio Art from Trinity University in San Antonio.

Ansen is now a 53-year-old commercial and art photographer in San Antonio, where he stayed after his "second" degree. He and his wife Doerte, a native of Germany, have one son, Luca, who has recently graduated from college in Scotland. Ansen's photographic images have been well received, with many showings in Texas as well as in such places as Chicago, Los Angeles, China, and the Canary Islands.

With a mind toward speculation and invention, Ansen invented a device called a slit-scan camera which records only slivers of objects passing in front of it. This results in beautifully or grotesquely distorted images. As for music, Ansen was a proficient trombonist in high school and college, and has continued to play in ensembles as an adult. There will be more in a later chapter on Ansen's life work, but for now, these few facts about him can serve as a backdrop as we return to his beginning.

If a child is born to a couple with genetic predispositions toward creativity, what occurred in the nurture department to enhance those leanings? When Ansen was born on Dec. 12,1960, in the McAllen Municipal Hospital, we had not played Mozart and Bach intentionally to his unborn self. But let the record show, for whatever it might be worth, that during that nine months, I played the flute in the Pan American Symphony Orchestra and attended most of the concerts performed in the Lower Rio Grande Valley of Texas where we lived.

The Sunday before his birth in the night, I went to church and took communion, attended a rehearsal of Handel's *Messiah* that afternoon, fixed dinner for a couple of friends, and to top it off, went to a movie. No wonder Ansen came barreling into the world with scarcely three hours' notice.

We were living in a drafty old rent house with gas wall outlets for space heaters. Carl had to go buy a stove before Ansen and I came home from the hospital. It was the smallest, least expensive one on the market and only heated our bedroom. I remember coming home from the hospital, babe in arms, and walking through the cold house to the closed door of the bedroom.

When Carl opened the door, a lovely waft of warm air greeted the baby and me. And twirling from the ceiling light fixture was a large red papier-mâché goose with wings outspread, fluttering with dangling crepe paper strips. Carl took Ansen in his arms and held him up to the bird. "See this, baby?" he said. "This is your very own Fire-bird." It seems Carl had been passing by the local piñata maker and had bought it, probably with the pocket change from the space heater, as a home-coming gift to the baby, inspired by Stravinsky's "The Fire-bird Suite."

The baby's hands came up in a start and his newborn eyes tried their best to focus. It wasn't exactly a crib toy but it stayed there for many weeks, entertaining the baby as it turned slowly in the rising heat from the tiny space heater.

I doubt that it had any artistic effect on the child, but who knows? Recent research has revealed that newborns have marvelous powers of discernment. So what might have been the far-reaching effects of a twirling red goose?

One of the most valuable legacies from my mother was a large brown envelope stuffed with the letters I had written to my parents when the boys were small. Living several hundred miles from them, and on a tight teachers' budget, we relied mostly on letters to communicate with them. Reading those letters a half-century later, I see now that we were the typical first-time parents and Ansen was the typical first-born. He had our undivided attention.

There was that good strong general obsession of two adults focused on the development of a small child. What were some of the hallmarks, early on, that he would become a creator and make a life for himself in the arts? How can we ever know? But here are some examples from his early personality as recorded in my letters:

Ansen at 22 months: "Yesterday we were eating carrots for lunch. He took one, held it out to me and said, 'Here, rabbit!'"

"Everything with him now is, 'Ready? Jump!' or 'Ready? Go!'"

"When I told him at the grocery store that he could have some candy when we got home, he said plaintively, 'But Mommy, I'll surely starve'—words straight out of *Hansel and Gretel.*"

"In his little ABC book, he can fill in the last word of each line in the entire book. He can repeat all the letters in the alphabet and count up to 20. He sings, "Nigh, Nigh..' to 'Brahms Lullaby' and on the right pitches."

"Ansen said, 'We have to have an entrance and an outrance.'"

"We were decorating the Christmas tree when Ansen came to me, 'Mother, can you unstrangle these icicles?'"

When he was four, I write: "Ansen plays outside all day every day. It really goes hard with him when he has to stay in." Ansen's adult ability to invent and explore is evident in my comment when Ansen was four that "I have tied the strings, cut the holes, blown the balloons, fixed the Superman, glued the ripped, sewed the torn all week."

At this time, we were still television-less. We had one paperback Dr. Spock baby care book. Compared to the wealth of information sources today, we were mostly winging parenthood. We talked to him and hugged and kissed him a lot. And as he grew and began to stretch his boundaries, we watched and encouraged, or discouraged, even with a swat on the diapered behind, when he overstepped.

In the letters home, I describe three games Ansen devised, which would today be termed "unstructured play" or "free time":

"Box: Sometimes he plays for an hour in a big cardboard carton. There are all sorts of variations on this such as, 'Nigh, Nigh,' 'Peek-a-boo!' 'Kee-ko Nigh, Nigh' and 'Dark! Dark!'" In 20/20 hindsight, we could whimsically wonder if this last one was a precursor of his later photographic darkrooms.

"The Physically Handicapped Game: This game also has many facets but the main one is pretending he's blind. He covers his eyes with his hands and goes around tenderly bumping into doors and furniture all the while grinning like a possum. He also pinches his throat when he eats to see how hard he can pinch before he chokes. And he puts his thumb on his eyeball and rubs it back and forth until it's so red we have to make him quit."

"The Weed Game: He 'weeds' everything now that looks as if it might have print on it. He will get a piece of music, lie down on the floor, hold it up close to his face, and say, "Seex, three, C, Hi, Good, 'member, four-five-seex,' and with a final sigh, 'hay-kay' (okay)."

Here's an original poem Ansen said to me when he was three:

Fly, fly, butterfly!
Oh so high!
I wish you would come down
back to bounds.

Ansen was a questioner of the first degree and that trait has carried over into his life's work in experimental photography. When he was five years old, I recorded his inquiries in the car on the way home one night:

"Why are there two men on the back of a fire truck?"

"Do fire trucks stop for red lights?" (Then he answered it himself with "Yes, they stop coming back from a fire but they don't stop going to one.")

"How do bridges get built if there's water all under them?"

"Do women box?"

"Do the football boys' pants lace up over their tinklers?"

"What does 'desire' mean?"

"I see twelve, no....nineteen stars."

"Do football players march in the band too?"

But I get ahead. When Ansen was two-and-a-half, and when we had lavished much attention on him as the first-born, another boy showed up. In June of 1963, Ansen was joined by his brother Erren Clint.

Replicating Ourselves: Erren

Erren Clint was born the afternoon of June 11, 1963 in Valley Baptist Hospital in Harlingen. Carl was the band director at Harlingen High School and I had managed to teach sophomore English at Harlingen High School for one year before Erren's birth. We brought Erren home to a modest tract house, somewhat more comfortable than the house we brought Ansen to as a baby in Edinburg.

Erren is now a 51-year-old businessman with co-ownership of a popular antiques and cultural arts retail store, VIDA, in McAllen. He lives with his partner Fernando Rivera in a 1929 Spanish, California-revival style house in central McAllen. Erren holds a Bachelor of Fine Arts degree from the University of Texas at Austin.

For some years after he graduated, he worked as a graphic designer in Austin, Houston, and the Valley. After winning a number of regional, state, and national awards for his design work, he chose to close his design studio and become a retail merchant. VIDA draws shoppers from the Valley, northern Mexico, and the Southwest to buy unusual chests, tables, carved gates, altar pieces, and iconic art imports from around the world. Erren cherishes McAllen's history and promotes preservation of both architectural and natural features of the area.

As a toddler, Erren showed an interest in music, drama, and art. In one of my letters home when he was two, I comment to my parents, "Erren accepted the records [children's songs on disk they had sent] with a wonderful smile. All he has wanted to do is listen to the record player these two weeks—and I really can't see much wrong with that!"

When he was three-and-a-half, I report, "Right now Erren is dancing around the living room to Tijuana Brass. He is just wild with imagination. He dreams, plays, jabbers, dances all the day."

Also at that time, he became interested in the story and music of *The Sound of Music*. He drew pictures of all the principals, and sang and danced to the songs. In one drawing he even depicted the RCA dog on the record label.

His favorite holiday was Halloween. An early drawing was of a witch, with a notation in my handwriting that he called her hat "her spout." In the first grade, he wrote a poem:

> Have you seen any gost at all
> I've seen some, have you?
> Oh yes! Oh yes! I've seen some.
> I am one.

All Erren's writing was accompanied by drawings, and this one has a detailed "gost," with eyebrows and eyes with pupils, and a bat flying by.

A song Erren composed and lavishly illustrated with pumpkin and witch was notated for him by his father on music manuscript paper. The lyrics were

> Ten white skeletons walking down the street
> knocking on the doors for trick or treats.
> Eight black witches are saying heh, heh, heh,
> Saying heh, heh, heh,
> Come catch me if you dare.
> Two white ghosts are saying woo, woo, woo,
> Saying woo, woo, woo, woooo, woooo!

Lots of heh-hehs and woo-woos, but I think it's significant that Carl stopped to take down the tune and words Erren dictated to him. It's typical that we knew no better than to pay them serious attention for their creative efforts.

Erren's preoccupation with art is apparent in the volume of his drawings. In one letter, I tell my parents, "Erren averages 15 to 20 pictures a day. He draws on any sheet available, usually the backs of papers Carl and I are finished with." He didn't favor any kind of drawing implement over another but used just whatever was available—ballpoint pen, pencil, or crayon.

By the time he went to kindergarten, his pictures filled the page and were lavish with detail and color. Men's suits were double-breasted, women wore matching hair bows and high heels, and cats played violins. In one picture, drawn at five and titled by Erren "Queen and

Tornado," the red-haired queen sporting a golden crown raises her lavender arms in dismay as a green funnel cloud dips down toward her. Nearby a tree tosses with rain and lightning.

Theatre was entering his life about this time. While we were in graduate school in Denton, Erren was chosen to sing the role of the Child Nicholas in Benjamin Britten's *Life of Nicholas* and was picked as the changeling for Shakespeare's *Midsummer Night's Dream.*

A pencil drawing I saved was obviously drawn on a church bulletin when Erren was five. (Yes, it was a time when children who were five were considered old enough to sit quietly with their parents through an hour of church.) In the drawing, an alarmingly happy Christ is stretched on a cross, with a coiffed, beskirted Mary beneath, along with the crosses of the two criminals. But in the foreground, that's where the action really picks up. There, on an extended sidewalk, is a series of Easter bunnies, with the lead bunny carrying an egg basket. On either side of the walkway stands a phalanx of Christmas trees, heavy with Easter eggs. The adjoining page contains the printed order of worship, superimposed on which is obviously the writing of the older patient brother Ansen: "EASTER THIS IS WHHT ITS ALL ABOUT."

As for the brotherly dynamics of Ansen and Erren, they played well together and were loyal and protective of each other. Illustrating this is an episode that will always remain in my heart.

When Erren was three, I began to teach again at Harlingen High School. At that time, there were few daycare places, and I managed to talk a church friend with small children into keeping my two, but mid-year she had to curtail her activities and I was forced to enroll the boys in a daycare facility.

This particular one had cyclone-fenced separate play areas for older and younger kids. One afternoon I was a little late picking Ansen and Erren up and found them standing beside each other on opposite sides of the dividing fence. It was obvious that Erren had been crying for a while. Ansen, now five, had run his arm through the fence and was holding Erren's hand, talking to him, assuring him Mom would be there soon. I vowed then that I would try to find another private home for them so they could be together.

An entry in my letter writing details another connection. "Ansen read his first book today. He just lay down on the kitchen floor with Erren, said, 'Erren, I'll read it to you.' And away he went. He would actually jump up and down while he was turning the page. He was so happy to be doing it all himself at last."

This behavior was to be mirrored later on when Erren was the big brother to the third son, Avrel. Thank heavens for brothers!

Erren was particularly sensitive to whatever Carl and I were interested in at home. If we listened to Hal Holbrook's *Mark Twain Tonight*, Erren was right there listening too. When he was in the third grade, we acquired and listened to, with great merriment, the composer Peter Schickele's "The Stoned Guest: A Half-Act Opera" on a 33 1/3 LP. It is a sophisticated take-off on classical music and we laughed so hard we cried. As young children will, Erren picked up on our laughter, and though I'm sure he didn't quite understand all the humor, he asked to take it to school to play for his classmates as his show-and-tell. We agreed, reluctantly; after all, the humor was somewhat dependent on a listener's concert experience. When he came home that afternoon, he was really angry. It seems his classmates had talked during the playing of the funny music, not appreciating the humor at all. Erren was sorely disappointed. He had had a bad experience with music appreciation.

When Erren was in the fourth grade, we took the family to Washington, D.C. and in the National Gallery he saw the series of paintings by the American painter Thomas Cole called "The Voyage of Life," which depicts the seasons of the year as the voyager rides on a boat through the American wilderness. Erren was really taken with this and decided to buy the postcards of it. He took them home and displayed them in his room. That was the year, 1973, when, conscious of the various mediums of graphic art by this time, he quipped one day, "I guess I shouldn't be oil painting if there's an energy crisis."

Although visual art was ever on his mind, he could be a wordsmith too. Here he writes a poem:

Seahorses

As a knight of water chess
I see him make a move
to a nearby seaweed garden.
The eel calls a check-mate.
Then the pieces swim away.

So did his childhood.

Another Seale Pup: Avrel

When Avrel came into the world in late January of 1967, we put out a birth announcement that read,

> Another Seale pup showed up.
> We kept him as a pet
> and called him Avrel Bret.

Avrel is now a 47-year-old communications professional and freelance writer. His career for seventeen years was as editor of *The Alcalde*, the magazine for The University of Texas at Austin 91,000-member alumni association. Now he is the speech writer for the president of the university. Because the university is one of the largest major research universities in the nation, in any given week, Avrel may be involved with all sorts of social, scientific, educational and cultural events that require his own research and quick response.

Avrel lives with his wife Kirstin and their three young sons in Austin.

Avrel plays the guitar, violin, and piano for relaxation, and occasionally performs in public, but his principal outlet for artistry is in his writing, which luckily blends with his day job. As if he needed a busman's holiday, he has authored eight books—on his lunch hour, evenings, and weekends. These include two memoirs, four books with a philosophical-spiritual premise, a children's book, and a book on Texas history.

The timing of Avrel's birth coincided with a transition in our lives. Carl had decided he no longer wanted to be a band director. His musical interests had always been serious and high school band directing involved too many parades and half-time shows. In late spring of 1967, he was accepted into the doctoral program in music at North Texas State University. So in August, we left our beautiful new home outside Harlingen, the house we had brought newborn Avrel home to earlier in the year, and made our way to Denton with a seven month old, a four year old, and a six year old.

There we lived in a small cramped rent house on a very tight budget. Carl began his doctoral studies, became director of the Denton High School Orchestra and took a job as choir director of a church. I tended the boys and the home, and began taking night classes on my master's. Is it any wonder that I don't have a list of darling clever acts and utterances of the young Avrel? I have had to forgive myself for not keeping a journal at this time.

Certainly Avrel walked and talked on time, and did cute things, but numbers do make a difference and I simply didn't have the time to record him as I had my first- and second-born. Also, there are not many letters of mine from the first four years of Avrel's life because we lived closer to my parents, who lived in Oklahoma, and visited them in person more often.

Avrel loved pranks and was, as a toddler, perhaps the most daring of our three boys. That probably follows a pattern in families with multiple children. The first child is hovered over unduly, the second completes a pair that can be tidily governed, and the third child—three's a crowd and things have gone chaotic—is on his own.

It wasn't surprising to find him on top of the piano, in the upper bunk bed, or hidden in a closet. One day I looked out and saw our toddler squatted behind the horse which was pastured in a small lot behind our house. Avrel was gazing intently at one hoof. He had slipped through the fence when I'd looked away for a minute.

When he was two, we went back to the Valley to spend Easter break with Carl's parents in La Feria. They lived on North Parker Road where their 10 initial acres had been bisected by Expressway 83 so that there was only one field between their house and the highway. In the early evening of Maundy Thursday we were getting ready to attend church services when we heard the yells of a young child in the field. Rushing out, we found that Avrel had slipped out of the house and was headed across the furrows directly into the line of traffic. Erren had seen him and bolted after him. He couldn't persuade Avrel to come back so he had simply lain down on him there in the furrow and begun screaming at the top of his voice for someone to come rescue them. Again, thank heavens for brothers!

Avrel loved to dress up in costumes and play various hero figures.

Once, after viewing *The Three Musketeers*, Avrel came into the kitchen dressed as a musketeer. He drew his plastic baseball bat sword on me and called out loudly, "Mother! Crochét!"

Before Avrel could read and write, Erren would help him to make books. Avrel had a story concocted in his head and wanted badly to record it, so Erren would write the story for him and illustrate it. The pages of these "books" were usually second sheets, printed on one side with Carl's and my class materials. We kept a number of these, and they have an interesting function now, showing the little boys' storytelling and art, and Carl's and my work projects at one and the same turn-through. I don't ever remember the children fussing about not having nice paper to compose on. They were too busy with their creations to care.

Avrel's light really began to shine when he reached school age. He couldn't get enough of learning, but he wanted to do it his way. When he was in third grade, he announced, "School is bad for your mind." He would relentlessly pursue a subject that interested him until he had it down pat, regardless of what he was *supposed* to be learning at the time.

He focused in on a subject to the distraction of the entire family. We had to learn it in all its detail along with him. The whole family became versed in dinosaurs and whales, in American patriots and rock formations, in Vikings and ancient weapons.

Avrel loved making lists. One afternoon I was driving the station wagon loaded with carpooling kids, the housekeeper was speaking rapid Spanish to me, and we were in the midst of heavy traffic, when Avrel called sweetly from the far back seat, "Mom, want to hear the names of George Washington's dogs?"

Avrel early on showed a philosophical bent. When he was eight, he averred, "I wish civilization hadn't ruined everything." One afternoon after a hard day at school, when his friend Susan, the other scholar in the class, had beaten him once again on a test score, he came dejectedly into the kitchen and slumped at the table. With quivering voice, he said sadly, "I know what's going to happen, Mother, I really do." That was my cue. "What's going to happen?" I stirred the rice.

Avrel studied his hands and swallowed. Tears filled his eyes. "The girls are just going to get better and better until they take over the world."

He was always ready to fashion things from homemade materials rather than buy them. Once when we were preparing for a birthday party for him, I explained what party favors were, and told him we needed to have them on hand and ready for the big day. He replied, "Oh, good. I'll get busy making them right now." And he did. He also insisted on making valentines for his entire class. From these long sessions at the dining table I was able later to glean the major premise of a much-published short story, "Jack of Hearts."

Soon after Avrel entered public school, he began to draw with zeal and intensity. Although he had long been exposed to Erren's finely detailed contemporary scenes, Avrel often chose to concentrate on historical figures, such as drawing busts of George Washington and Alexander Hamilton. He distinguished himself as the class artist and was invited at times to draw large scenes on the blackboard, a request he relished. Once, he and I were discussing what "medium" was as related to art, and he said, "You will know the medium by the kind of idea you have."

His love of drawing lasted until the fourth grade, when Avrel became acutely dissatisfied with his art work, tearing up half-done endeavors and going off in a black mood. This disturbed time was right on schedule for a phenomenon I only learned about later. The corpus callosum, which is the large rope-like band connecting the two sides of the brain, is finally solidified at about age 10. Before that time, the right brain, which promotes creativity, dreams, and general wool-gathering, is a fairly free agent, allowing the child to move about in imaginative play without critical self-analysis.

When the right brain is totally connected to the left brain, which flexes itself in rules and reasoning, there are new signals telling the right brain that this or that idea is silly, socially unacceptable, maybe flat wrong. We can see how this phenomenon can stifle creativity in a child. It may be that only those children with strong beliefs in their creativity, who have the drive and get great pleasure out of "making things," will grow into adult creators. Fortunately, Avrel had other artistic pursuits in mind, notably music and writing, which began to bloom as he hit adolescence.

Avrel's third grade coincided with the bicentennial of the USA in 1976. His teacher brilliantly encouraged her class in American history that year. Avrel literally became John Hancock, dressing in Colonial wear and copying Hancock's famous signature on various documents around the house.

From the get-go, Avrel manifested a high degree of individuality. He says of his early sense of self, "I don't think I felt different, but I can see very clearly in retrospect the eccentricities."

He was not hampered by reality. Once he staged a full boxing match between himself and a neighbor child in the backyard, complete with roped ring and tickets for the onlookers. I watched from the kitchen, coming within a nanosecond of rushing out to save him from the bigger boy.

Another time, he decided to have his own Oberammergau on a nearby vacant lot. After Avrel assigned the neighborhood children their parts and pled with his father to take a role, Carl told him emphatically that, No, he would not be Christ on the cross. (Thirty years later, Avrel was able to cast his father in a "play," this time a part in his feature-length indie film, *The Secret of Suranesh,* his account of which is in the Appendix.)

We had many a laugh and a few head-shakings at Avrel's young idiosyncratic personality. In a letter to us from college, he wrote, "You made me converse over a sit-down dinner every night, you encouraged me to take typing in the 8th grade, you provided me with encyclopedias and you let me whittle wooden swords in the back yard, i.e. be weird."

Permit me to end this chapter with a poem I wrote about him during his childhood:

Crack of Dawn

I found you
one morning
awake too early,
coiled in your covers
against the chill,
your drawing tablet,
a pencil, the "L"
of the encyclopedia.
My son,
did anyone ever tell you
eight year olds
in America

do not sketch
from Leonardo
on cold mornings?
No one has given you
instructions
for shaping the aquiline nose,
shading the *sfumato*.
You are
a sketchbook intact,
a flying machine,
a Milanese horse,
a Florentine sundial.
You are the reason
behind my enigmatic smile.[1]

Part Two: Glimpses

Introduction

In 1994, Avrel was being interviewed on the Lee Hibbetts Show at radio station KURV. The interviewer queried, "How was it growing up in a creative family?" Avrel's answer: "Like a traveling circus act!"

Today I listened to a cassette tape made in 1972 for the grandparents. (Thank you, Mother, for preserving it.) Avrel, 7, read a poem I had written for him entitled "Avrel, the Reader." It was a little over his reading level and he'd stop and say earnestly, "Excuse me just a minute while I find my place."

Erren, 9, sang a song he had composed, "I Know a Place," accompanying himself on the piano. He describes his ideal place in several stanzas, where "We can spend our hours/ in calm and warm sunshine."

Ansen, 12, is beginning to self-censor. He says his first piece played on his trombone will be "Alma Mater" and after he's played it, he wryly announces that that's his last piece also, since he doesn't have another prepared.

To hear our boys speaking as they did 41 years ago fills me with awe for the technology. More than that, it fills me with maternal yearning for their lost childhoods. Their soft solemn little voices, explaining to their grandparents what they are about to do, are tinged with self-consciousness. They don't seem to be showing out. They're just sharing what they've been doing with themselves lately—poems, stories, songs, tunes.

Of course, they were also busy with other sorts of ordinary boy things. The following is a random offering of life in our family during their boyhoods. The first essay, "The Pursuit of Happiness," is excerpted from my book titled *Homeland*. Those short pieces following are adapted from columns I wrote under the title "Living and Other Complications" in the McAllen-based *Town Crier;* thus the point of view is that of the contemporary mother of young boys.

Are there things peculiar that made a difference in our children's career choices and lifetime exercise of creativity? Maybe. I leave it to the reader to decide by these slices of family life.

The Pursuit of Happiness

It was the summer of '71 and we were on the road in the Pursuit of Happiness. We had three little boys, the biggest rental truck available filled with Early Marriage furniture, $700 in cash, and a crazy idea: Get back to the Rio Grande Valley in south Texas.

My husband had spent his high school years in La Feria, a little town in the mid-Valley, and the region was in his blood. When we graduated from the University of Louisville, he brought me back for a year in Edinburg and six in Harlingen. Then we moved away, upstate, to get some more education, agreeing that we probably would never return to the Valley to live. Too remote. Too provincial. Thanks but no thanks.

But four years and two degrees later, we discovered we'd exchanged orchards for used car lots, palm trees for security lights, and "God- how'dyoudoit?" sunsets for urban pall.

One night, amidst dossiers and phone calls, we made a list, like Ben Franklin recommended, of what we wanted in a locale: green grass, friendly folk—but not too many, moderate climate, clean air, a good school system, things to do. Oh yes, and space.

"Do you know where this is?" we sheepishly asked ourselves. So this was how we came to be caravanning to the Valley, looking like the Joads from *The Grapes of Wrath,* convinced we could eventually make a living for ourselves in our music and writing professions if we zeroed in on the right environment.

Once here, we began a tour of the countryside between McAllen and Edinburg looking for a farmhouse someone wanted to let us live in, preferably for nothing. With all our worldly goods simmering in the parked rental truck, our little boys whining and fidgeting in the back seat of the car, and nothing more than blind faith, we systematically crisscrossed north to south from Highway 107 to a dirt road known as

Nolana on the north outskirts of McAllen, and then east to west from McColl Road to Ware Road.

The third day, we found a painter sprucing up an old farm dwelling on Minnesota Road. As the boys headed for the nearest irrigation standpipe, we learned that the owners, who lived up north, were planning to rent the place. We declared ourselves prospects and took the tour. The room called the bathroom housed only an old freestanding tub. The room known as the kitchen could be recognized by a hole in the wall where the sink pipe had once been. In the hallway, a little girl named Irma had immortalized herself with a signed self-portrait. The place would need a lot of work.

But outside, the boys had already begun a game of hide-and-seek in the forty-acre orange grove. So what could we do?

We got the owners' number and a few days later moved in, having reached an agreement that we would renovate the interior in exchange for several months' rent.

That next week, the older boys went to school at Jackson Elementary in McAllen. But it rained that first day of September, as it did every other day that month in 1971, and so we had to drive them in a square: east on Minnesota, south on McColl, and back west on La Vista. Between us and the school was a huge impassable pond.

Somehow we got through that year. We figured out how to get water from the canal, and then how to purify it enough to take a bath in it. We memorized the schedule of the ditchrider, for he was the one who determined when we washed our clothes and filled our reservoir. After the signal from him, Carl would climb the standpipe out front and turn the wheel inside to release water into our tank.

We installed a kitchen sink and a bathroom toilet. Then we sanded floors and paneled walls (Goodbye, Saint Irma of the hallway). When a norther blew in, we noticed that we didn't have any means to heat the house, so we had to talk our landlords into installing a butane system.

We killed rats by the dozen and roaches by the hundred. We routed possums from beneath the house and challenged raccoons in the attic. Were we having fun yet? Was this the Pursuit of Happiness?

Meanwhile, our little boys made friends with an old guinea hen roosting in the orchard. "Coquena" shared the orchard with a remarkably shy English sheep dog who darted in and out among the waxy leaves of the orange trees and thus earned the name of "Creep."

The boys rode the palm trees in our front yard that had been felled by some past hurricane and had partially uprighted themselves. They chased wild parrots and ate oranges, or tangerines—the tree of which, one son tells me now, they located by counting ten rows over from the house and three back from the road.

They had a fondness for wading in a deep ditch by the standpipe, developed a loving friendship with a pony pastured at the corner of 2nd and Minnesota, and kept track of a nest of quail in a nearby field. One son filled his entire lunchbox with baby frogs one afternoon on the walk from the bus stop.

That year we gleaned vegetables from already-harvested fields and from right-of-way spills. We picked carrots, by permission, from a field behind the orchard and grew greens in a garden. Every morning we had ten-minute-old orange juice. We ate dates from the palms and had mulberry pie from an ancient tree behind us.

In addition to these measures, we kept our bills paid by substitute teaching in school districts all around. For a long time after-ward, my husband was greeted with "Hi, Coachie!" from little boys on the street.

Meanwhile, we had all made "town" friends, and, when spring came around, we began to have a virtual parade of folk, walking, cycling, or driving out from town on weekends and holidays. They'd stand in the yard and call softly until one of us noticed them. Assured of our wel-come, the adults flopped in the grass under the mesquites with coffee while their kids took off with ours to the orchard. Yes, we were having fun yet.

The Fourth of July. People asked shyly what we might be doing that day. They might come out. We decided to get organized. We'd cook the meat if everyone else brought a dish. So, on our spidery, rickety screened-in porch a table was laid fit for the gods. Amid the few patriotic trappings we could scour up as decorations, our friends placed deviled eggs and potato salad and beans and homemade bread and sliced garden tomatoes and brownies and coconut cake. And at dusk, in the yard—the old holey, burr-ridden, uneven yard—we set out our lawn chairs, flapped down quilts for the kids, and ate homemade mango ice cream, watching across the groves as fireworks whooshed up from McAllen.

Not too long after that, the place was sold and we were forced to move and buy a house in town. The boys pled with their dad to take the tree house "in." No, boys, there are rules in town. Creep must be left behind, for an orchard dog would never be happy in town. And now we had to buy our oranges at the roadside stand like everyone else.

Even yet we dream of that little Eden. In one of my dreams, the house becomes available again and we move back. We occasionally still declare periods of mourning where we opine that we were not allowed to stay on, reveling in the locale, building on our initial hard-won efforts.

Where the forty acres of orange trees grew, a subdivision bloomed, complete with underground utilities, tree saplings, and curbs. Minnesota Road was renamed a flower street, Violet. But in an eerie architectural afterlife, our old farmhouse lived on for several years, encircled by fine brick homes with pools and fences and recessed garbage cans.

Finally, it came down one day, and in its place is a huge multi-gabled palatial home with a ten-foot cinder block wall around it. We never see any activity when we go by it, and we wonder if it's owned by some out-of-towners. Everything we can see is painted a bold beige—the gables, the wall, and, because the new owners couldn't remove it, "our" beloved huge irrigation standpipe at the driveway's edge.

Back toward town, a townhouse development sits where the quail's nest was, and the pony's lovely pasture is just a vacant lot reserved for maintenance equipment and utility installations.

Along with dreaming of it, we often laugh at ourselves for sentimentalizing a place so hopelessly old and rundown, and remember how backbreaking the work was to redeem it from decrepitude. We marvel that we had the nerve, the energy to attempt something so preposterous. We would never begin such a thing now, but the experience gave us—as our grandmothers would say—starch.

In a paradoxical way, we're resentful that so many people shared our common dream—to come to the Valley and enjoy a good quality of life, resentful because now we no longer have our Eden, even though, long before the town grew north, we had become one of the "town" people ourselves.

But here is the point: we had the freedom to *become*. We were allowed to choose, over and over and over. To return to the Valley. To realize a country-living fantasy. To educate our children in the local

36

schools. To seek our niche in the workplace. Our best selves call us to grant that right to others, knowing that *preserving* the freedom must take priority over *claiming* it.

Here in America we may rise and gather our children about us and strike out. With lightning swiftness, we repitch our tents, gamble our possessions, seek new friends, claim our priorities. All this with the backing of the Ninth Amendment, which says that we can do whatever we please unless it's expressly forbidden by law. In other words, Pursue Happiness.

In our family's pursuit, we long ago surrendered the old 30's farmhouse on Minnesota Road to "progress"—our own and everyone else's. Still, it's fun to remember how we brought the stereo out to the creaky wooden porch that Fourth of July back in 1972 and had an afternoon of stirring Sousa marches, as loud as we wanted them, with hundreds of orange trees listening.

The Bookends of a School Day

Why must every day have a set of bookends, morning and night? Either side is a trauma for a mother. It isn't that any of the tasks are so arduous; it's that there are so many of them.

Take for example, this morning. Nobody but another mother would believe that between 6:30 and 8:00, I did the following:

-operated on an ingrown toenail
-covered an English textbook
-dried a tennis shoe with the hair dryer
-re-labeled a pair of P.E. shorts
-heard reasons why a boy should wear to school a giant-size orange t-shirt with chicken blood fishing bait stains on it
-vetoed all the reasons
-hunted for a book club ad
-filled a pocket-size bottle with sunflower seeds
-heard a story about a boy who ripped his pants on the playground
-complimented a boy that his hair was lying down nicely in back
-was told that he didn't want his hair to lie down nicely in back
-heard a long synopsis of a proposed short story modeled after *The Poseidon Adventure* and *The Towering Inferno* in which people are trapped in a building during a flood.

Is it any wonder their cherubic Bye, Moms fill me with maternal joy? Now I have twelve hours to get my head on straight before the nightly rituals.

About 8 p.m., when I'm longing to sink into an easy chair and read last Sunday's paper, it's time to...
-haul a lieutenant in the ape corps down from a mesquite tree
-read a library book due tomorrow
-set the clock for an early student council meeting

-find the toothpaste
-hear reasons one should not get a haircut
-give a haircut
-listen to a list of body locations where one can contract athlete's
 foot from the showers at school
-look at a soaped cavorting dragon in the bath tub
-learn that one boy is "double-jointed in the eyes"
-hunt for a metal car, which is tonight's comfy object
-settle a fight over whose turn it is for the dog to sleep with them
-sing both the melody and harmony to all stanzas of "Ivy Twine"
-settle a fight over a threat to reveal the ID of a brother's girlfriend
-put a bicycle, a pogo stick, and a bag of rocks in the garage.

The first round is over. Nine o'clock. I sink into my chair with a glass of tea, murmuring something meaningful like hello to my husband. The little one's voice wafts from his room. I set my glass aside. The newspaper slides from my lap. I pad to the doorway. Carefully checking my desire to scream, I say, "Son, it's time to go to sleep."

"I know," he replies. "I'm just talking myself over."

National Association Against Projects
of Paper and Tape
(a tongue-in-cheek protest of child creativity)

There ought to be an organized effort against all projects by children involving paper and tape. Such a group would have three goals: to fight frustration in children, to fight parents' urges to kill, and to cut down on the wasteful consumption of paper and tape.

Until now, nothing has been done to curb projects of paper and tape. If anything, well-meaning child psychologists have only made the problem worse by telling adults they should encourage children in all their creative efforts. The experts have failed to exclude paper and tape.

A child has a blind trust in these deceptive desk tools. Once, before we could stop him, one of our children created an entire rock collection by taping rocks to pieces of paper. There's a logistics problem when a child tapes a four-pound boulder from a nearby field to a piece of typing paper.

Then there was another project consisting of a large box constructed out of flimsy paper and tape. It kept dying when it was supposed to be dimensional. It kept collapsing when it should be cubing. It brought on a bad bout of tears and self-loathing, the final humiliation being that it was put in the trash when someone thought the dog had brought it in.

Every Halloween, we suffered the torments of a mask made out of notebook paper, to be attached to the head with string or elastic. The mask maker confidently put it on, and it confidently ripped out before he could get to the mirror. No amount of foot-stamping would make it a workable creation.

And who wants to say cruelly, "You failed. Throw it away"?

Not this mother. So I got up from my easy chair and went looking for the little round reinforcements. But the bugs had eaten the glue off them, so I spent a while patching the holes with...tape. This time the fasteners didn't rip out until *after* the child had gotten to see his scary visage in the mirror.

We ended up trying to find an all-night drugstore that sold our child's creative idea, a Draculian astronaut mask.

As for tape, children think of it as a panacea. Once, a full yard of sticky tape was used to laminate a newspaper photo of a lost puppy. Another time, a budding carpenter managed to shanghai a whole roll of tape in place of a nail to connect two 2x4s. Then there was the incident when one of the boys tried to immolate himself by taping up all the body orifices. And when a slingshot made with ice cream sticks and tape was activated, it broke apart so fast that one of the sticks beat the rock to the target.

As for paper, think of all the paper boats, hats and snowflakes lying behind the couches of America. Think of the fleets of paper fighter bombers idling under the nation's beds. Teachers, think of the little blow-up boxes with censorable remarks inside. Consider the triangular footballs, the sets of pinchers, the "Kick Me" signs placed surreptitiously on students' backs.

And think, think, everyone, of the galaxies of dried spitballs stuck to the ceilings of our world.

Are these not reasons far more than enough to mobilize? We can overcome. NAAPPTians, unite!

First Grade Dropout

I felt particularly glad for a summer break from school because I wasn't able to keep up with first grade that year. I'm a slow learner and I hoped my seven year old, Avrel, would forgive some of my intellectual inadequacies and allow me to go with him to second grade the next fall.

For one thing, I didn't know all the phonics rules. I got confused on whether the "g" before "i," "y," and "e" sounded like "guh" or "juh." I couldn't get straight what the double-dotted, polka-dotted "a" does, nor did I know all the silly ditties that would help in conquering short "i." According to my son, I was a phonics dropout.

Pronunciation was another problem area. I didn't know that a "heliocopler" is to fly around in, that a "fruitee-ator" is a cold box in the kitchen, that you blow your nose with a "hankerchip" and play a tune on the "pinano."

Meanings and facts eluded me also. I forgot that people can talk "sourcastic," that Nixon was one of Santa's reindeer, and that God is the only one that gets to stay home from church on Sunday. It was difficult for me to remember that your "intestament" is where your food goes after it leaves your stomach.

I didn't score very high on conduct either. I got two demerits from him for talking while I was in the bathroom. And one doesn't talk back to the official bathroom monitor that week at school.

The questions he posed that I couldn't answer were further proof of my poor showing. "How many minutes have I lived?" "Why is 'E' for Excellent when it's right next to 'F' for Failing?" "What color is a dog's heart?"

I failed the test in the nutrition field as well. I always thought I knew chopped onion when I saw it but my first grader informed me he didn't like plastic spice in his food. Neither did he care for rubber jelly (Jello, I surmised), or cow's eyelids—which, if you need a translation, is dried beef.

According to him I'd never excel in poetry either. I couldn't help that some of his verses left me cold. "So! So! Suck your toe/ All the way to Mexico!" seemed a bit intolerant to me. And, "Yankee Doodle went to town/ Riding on a turtle,/ Turned the corner on Highway One/ And saw a lady's girdle" struck me as less than immortal.

But I stayed cheerful and optimistic. I would have my post-first grader home for the summer as a private tutor. Perhaps, in fourteen hours a day, he could bring me up to second-grade level by the following September.

Operation Housepersons
(an open letter to the future life partners of my sons)

Dear lucky companions,

I have waiting for you some mates who are adept at household chores. They can do just about anything around the house, and as a result you and they should have very beautiful relationships.

I cannot let them go, however, without relating to you a little about the summer I trained them for their roles as housepersons.

It was 1974, and other women were doing campy things like marching for or against abortion, raising their consciousness levels, or standing around underwear bonfires. I had to be different. I chose to teach your mates, then ages 7, 11, and 13, how to do their part in the drudgery of housekeeping.

Their father (himself a partially liberated male) and I worked out the details. There would be bedmaking, dishwashing and sweeping daily. There would be dusting and mopping on Mondays and Thursdays, lawnmowing on Wednesdays, and dogbathing on alternate Saturdays. Smaller tasks would supplement these major ones.

The chart was posted on the kitchen wall. Each boy had a jar stocked with his week's allowance on the shelf. When a task was forgotten, a bit was subtracted and the task had to be done anyway. A family conference laid out the ground rules. All was agreed upon and the first Monday in June, Operation Housepersons began.

To appreciate what you are getting, I think you should realize that what they learned to do did not come easy—for them or me. Birds may know how to tidy their nests but it doesn't follow that humans have any instincts about housekeeping. There was no innate feeling in them to squeeze out the mop before they slid it across the floor. No instinctual yearnings whispered they should not dust the furniture with the dishrag. No law of the ages exerted itself in favor of hot dishwater over cold. They vacuumed only the middle of the floor. There was a cut-off point in their efficiency and desire, and nothing anyone said or did could make that point negotiable.

Sequencing was also a problem. One of you is getting a person, who, when he was seven, picked up the sticks in the yard *after* his brothers had mowed. Likewise, we had days when the sweeper swept *after* the mopper had mopped. And more than once, the drier stood with the cup towel twisted around his neck, whining because the washer for that day had deserted his post to go to his piano lesson.

Rotation of duties was also a bit touchy. Once, when the dog had prematurely and uncooperatively drunk her daily ration of water, we had to get out the calculator to determine whether tomorrow's pet wrangler should go on duty early or today's should work overtime.

One day, paper plates at noon seriously undermined the orderly ascent to the position of washer, and spilled raisins late one afternoon nearly required a labor-management negotiator.

The rule about forgetting one's task proved difficult to enforce. It didn't seem right to lose a dime and still have to do the task. Double jeopardy, sort of. I ended up as the Riddler, Mistress of Innuendo. If I said, "There is someone who needs to do something in the kitchen before something begins to smell and we can't get out the door," that meant the trash man had forgotten.

"I am looking at an object which has other objects moving on it" signaled the dog bather to get with it.

But we lived through the summer. We lived through a whole set of broken glasses, a water-logged kitchen floor, little colonies of spiders behind the drapes, a dining table awash with furniture polish. We lived through soapy rinse water and dried peas under the table. The dog lived through being thirsty.

And so, my dear future in-laws, I guarantee you companions with knacks, mates astute in mop and pail. But along with your partners, you'll have to take a mother-in-law who went slightly wacky during the summer of '74.

The Doggone First Grader: 1974

I used to think I was a pretty good first-grade mother. Back in 1967, I had simple worries with my neophyte Ansen, things such as getting him to wear corrective shoes, things such as apple or banana in the lunchbox and what to say to him the night before the tonsillectomy.

And then I practiced hard to be a good first-grade mom to Erren in 1969. I made cupcakes for the class and composed a poem which mentioned all his classmates by name.

But with the third child, mothering a first grader wasn't that simple. Take, for example, my experience as wardrobe mistress and stage manager for The Only Dancing Dog in Captivity, aka Avrel, said dog being a member of an acting company of policemen, dolls, cowboys, clowns, and butterflies from Room Three, First Grade at Jackson Elementary.

Avrel was a very picky first grader and so the costume couldn't be a pair of brown pajamas and a Halloween doggie mask. (Anyway, ever try to find a Halloween doggie mask in April?) It had to be authentic—everything but the bark.

I dragged out a vintage sewing pattern. It had already made a lion, a skeleton, and a rabbit with wire-lined ears. Unwittingly, I took it to the sewing shop. The sales clerk took one look at it and stammered, "Lady, where on earth did you get this pattern?"

"I'm sure I don't remember," I replied.

"Well, hang on to it," was her advice. "It's only thirty-five cents and it may already be a collector's item."

Home again with sewing materials, I methodically began on the genuine brown-with-white-spots doggie, complete with hood, ears, paws, and a spastically wagging tail. Seven hours later, I remembered this was no ordinary dog. This was a circus dog. So far, I had only made a dog hide. Now the outfit needed a red cone-shaped hat topped by a pompom, with a matching pleated neck ruff.

"Mom," my first grader began after giving me a rewarding kiss when he came from school that afternoon, "do you love me enough that you would make this costume if I asked you to make it for me just to play in?"

I swallowed hard, remembering that Dr. Spock wrote that children can sense lying parents. So I equivocated. "You know I would do anything at all that I thought you really needed."

"That means you wouldn't," he sang, and went off to the kitchen for a cookie.

Now The Only Dancing Dog in Captivity required a place to be captive, specifically a large cardboard box 29 ½ inches long to be mounted on a wagon and decorated with iron bars, blue paint, and curlicues of gold. Thinking the first graders would surely do everything left to right, my husband made a box with only one side adorned in the best tradition of Barnum and Bailey.

An aside here: Both of us parents were kindly disposed to this project. As a child, Carl was taken yearly to the circus when it came to Ft. Worth, where his mother's cousins, The Flying Beehees, performed on the high wire. And throughout my sister's and my childhood, she and I practiced on our backyard swing set to become trapeze artists in the Gainesville Community Circus. Just as Nan and I were getting good, really good at swinging by our legs from the crossbar, our father wisely found a different job in another town.

It was not until the dress rehearsal that we learned the wagon would be pulled not only left to right but right to left and down the middle. That night, strange mumblings and muffled oaths wafted from the garage. And the next morning at breakfast, I was afraid to say anything about the smudge of blue paint with the piece of imbedded glitter on my husband's nose.

Eleven hours of work for thirty seconds on stage! Isn't that some kind of formula expressing the ratio of most parents' work to their children's play?

But, in this case, oh what a thirty seconds! There's nothing to equal seeing a shy first grader become a cavorting, grinning, tail-wagging dog in front of three hundred people, pantomiming trickily to the tune of "How Much is that Doggie in the Window?"

Maybe, after all, it's a proper ratio.

The Last Fling of Summer

We went, probably the same as you, on a last fling before school started. We usually managed an overnight camp-out just up the country a few miles, at Falcon Lake.

That year, we got the outing accident over with before we even left. The little boy walked into the big boy's fish hook as they were packing the car. A major cry, some blood, a little scratch, several kisses —and we were on our way.

Our dachshund Taffy, dubbed the Brown Nuisance, went along. On camping trips, she managed to keep our affections on a roller coaster. We hated her when she bounded out of the car across a fresh tender scar on a boy's leg. We loved her when she kept on swimming, rhythmically, little front paws methodically treading and tail rotating like a helicopter blade—even when the boys lifted her high out of the water. We hated her when she slipped her collar in the night and we thought she had left camp. We loved her when she barked at a snake we stumbled on.

For this occasion, Carl made an exquisite campfire stew from scratch. At 9 p.m., he served our bowls, first going over to turn on the car lights. "Everybody take a good look at your plates!" he called, then snapped us into stew-eating darkness. We had forgotten the lantern.

I woke up three or four times in the night, once crawling out of the tent and gazing up at the shimmering, reeling, eternal ceiling. How could the speck-on-the-speck-meaning-me understand it all? I heard the coyotes crying, strong and willful, and felt glad there were still places one could hear wild things in the night.

The geometric lines of pink and blue in the pre-dawn sky caught the camp rabbits foraging around the garbage cans. The Brown Nuisance saw and grumbled but lay still, fascinated or outdone by the rabbits' hippity-hop audacity. A curve-billed thrasher came visiting for a stray corn chip.

That morning, we walked far down the shore. "Here it is!"

exclaimed Erren. "Here's my place, and I thought it was gone!" The gooey mud where we were walking had changed to a watery desert of untouched rippled sand. "This is the best feeling in the world," Erren crooned, watching his feet disappear in the silky shallows. He was light years away from upcoming books and pencils.

Then it was time to head home. The great-tailed grackles jawed about a leftover peanut-butter sandwich. Everyone was a little tired, a little sad at leaving, a little mixed up about going back home to the school year. The boys looked south to the gates of the dam. "There's the whole dam thing," quipped Ansen, with a twinkle in his eye that said he was for the moment semantically insulated against correction.

Erren was dreamily fingering an opalescent mussel shell. "Mother, if there is mother-of-pearl, is there father-of-pearl too?"

I think of the rabbits, the coyotes, the grackles, the Seales. "Why not?" I reply. "It sounds right to me."

Moving Day

The following piece was written not long after we moved from our old farmhouse north of McAllen to our present home in town.

Moving day is a moving experience, especially with three helpful children around. Recently we made a major move and I was fascinated by the way children's and grownups' minds differ under the circumstances. Contrasted to the zombie-like stance of my husband and me as we simply endured the event, the children's minds plumbed new depths of experience.

For one thing, their creativity was astounding. In one particular incident the movers had taken away the dining room chairs and were stalking back to begin work dismantling the large dining table. As they approached with their wrenches and dollies, they found our seven year old had moved on to the table with a "project." He had chosen this moment to begin a dinosaur mural. There he was with his thirty-six colored markers, two encyclopedias, and three feet of folding cardboard, smiling up at the burly truculent fellows. Times like these, a mother needn't worry about stifling her child's creativity. It's his *life* she needs to focus on.

Another trait that came out in the children was their love of animals. On our seventh trip house-to-house, with the car groaning under its load, our ten-year-old's passion for horses showed itself. While we were easing down a side street—large mirror bouncing dramatically on top of a pile of winter clothes, deck chair scratching the top, commode brush leering out the back window—our son screamed out.

I braked, prepared to see a scorpion whelp. "See that horse over there?" he cried, pointing to an animal tethered on an embankment. "Well, he's kicked his water over and he'll die if I don't get him some more *right now*!" I knew I couldn't win, so I pulled over.

The curiosity of children peaks at such critical junctures in family life. I love to answer questions about all sorts of things as I'm standing in the kitchen, varicose veins throbbing and system of homogeneous groupings broken down. Just when I'm wondering how to pack the dish drainer, a china cup, and the poisonous lye together, I get a question like "Where is my marble box?" or "Did you know there are six dogs in the house right now?"

It's like a jolt of electricity to hear, "Are you Grandmother's sister or mother?" or "What is that black on your cheek?" or "May I have my allowance for the last three weeks?"

Finally, I noticed the sociability of the children on moving day. They were certainly not preoccupied with material things. When all the beds had been removed from the old place, they begged to invite a few friends for a sleepover on the dust bunnies. They wanted to go swimming when their swim suits were in one—which one?—of forty-eight cardboard boxes. And at the new place, they found their skateboards and bicycles before I found the new house key and they made lifelong alliances with neighborhood children while we were wandering about the house deciding where to put the furniture.

It's the intangibles that were heavy on moving day. Thank heavens creativity, compassion, curiosity, and sociability can't be put in a box and tied down with string. How utterly prosaic and practical and adult-like.

Part Three: Presently

Introduction

Before attempting to categorize our sons' childhood influences, this seemed a good place to note the three of them in their midlife careers. Following their stories, I have taken the liberty to add Carl's and mine, with the hope of completing the picture of the family of adults. We were *there* for them as they grew up and left home, watching with bated breath but always with interest. Now they are *there* for us.

In a sense, this part is how we all grew up together.

Ansen: Art and Commercial Photography

When Ansen was five, he was dreaming over his cereal one morning. I asked him what he was thinking about. He said, "I wish I could get in a time machine." I pressed him a little and he explained he'd like to be back at his grandparents' house in Oklahoma, honking the horn of his grandfather's vintage Model T and taking walks down the street to look at yard art. These things occurred during an extended summer stay with them when he was not quite two years old.

And if we could have gone forward in a time machine, from that morning in 1965, we would have seen him as an adult still daydreaming about time, the result being experiments in photography that stand time and space on end. He is the inventor of a camera which uses a "slit-scan" process to record images. Contrary to panoramic cameras and video recorders, with this technique, the specially made camera remains still, recording whatever passes in front of the slit. Thus, still objects are blurred while moving bodies appear clear.

Ansen's patent for improvements to panoramic cameras was issued some thirteen years after the initial filing. And for twenty years, he has been experimenting with the slit-scan camera, with stunning images being chosen as cover art for books and journals, as well as shown in exhibitions and solo shows.

Ansen's interest in photography began in the ninth grade when he bought a used camera from a winter Texan, a basic 35 mm Pentax with no light meter. As a family, we were not much involved with taking photographs on vacations or of antics at home. Our photo albums prove we had a camera, but it was the simplest kind of point-and-shoot. Sometimes the roll of film stayed in the camera for weeks before we got around to getting it developed. So Ansen's interest in photography and his subsequent dedication to it as a life work came out of the blue. We parents did not realize how far he might take this hobby.

Ansen recalls, "There was a time when I knew that I had seen something that I wanted to record with a camera and that was pretty much it for me. There was a tree on 6th Street that was full of leaves and another that was dead just in front of it. It was like the one in front was showing the underlying structure of the one behind. When I finally bought my camera for $90 and made the shot some months later, I remember not being very satisfied with the result. But the whole technical process of getting the camera and learning to use it and developing the film had me hooked."

Here's a poem of mine addressed to Ansen during that period:

You Tell Me Your Dreams, I'll...

You said in the hall as we passed,
"In a little shrine high in the Himalayas
just off the main trail
and safe from rain and snow
will be all the things I've lost in life—
my lens cap and light meter,
my green shirt and the writing pen
with my name engraved." Breath.
"I'll just gather them up and go on to heaven in peace."

I was so astonished my son was going
to heaven via the Himalayas
I forgot I would have to sneak up
the night before, as on a Christmas eve,
to stock the place with years of searching.[1]

Jennifer James writes in her book *Defending Yourself Against Criticism* of The Lost Things Law: "A truly creative child will lose two jackets. . . . The creative person who lives his or her life up to its full potential will lose thousands of things."[2] A comfort to Ansen?

Writing of the origins of his life work, Ansen observes, "Now that I think about it, the impetus for that very first photo is still the main theme that I pursue in my work, the idea of an underlying reality and the passage of time. I'm sure a lot of that comes from reading science fiction as a teen and perhaps going to church. Also, being able to control the artistic process from start to finish was very important in my eventual decision to pursue photography as opposed to film or video."

Today Ansen heads a well-established business in San Antonio, Seale Studios, a commercial photography firm with three fulltime employees. His clients include a wide spectrum of entities, from heavy pipeline companies to other artists to socialites. In the beginning, the commercial shoots provided his entire livelihood but gradually, his personal art photography has gained him wide recognition and is economically on a par with his commercial photography.

"As a child I didn't think much about art," Ansen commented. "I remember thinking that the art crowd in high school was a bunch of loners. My identity was all in the band and JAAM."

When Ansen was a teen, he became a member of a charter group of Boy Scouts in a photography troop, sponsored by the father of one of the boys. Under this umbrella, Ansen's talent grew exponentially. The boys named themselves JAAM, for the first letters of their given names. They acquired an 8 mm movie camera—a cast-off of one of the parents—and began hanging out together to make films. One of the earliest ones they dubbed "Marching Bottles." It consisted of a group of Dr. Pepper bottles formed up into a marching unit on the street and through the magic of stop-action animation proceeding to miraculous formations, twists, and turns such as their own high school marching band might make. Today, we see such tricks all the time in computer animation, so it is remarkable that thirty-five years ago, these boys anticipated the technique with their marching bottles, waltzing garbage cans, and Monty Python-style antics. By the time they were seniors in high school, they had enough footage to offer an evening of entertainment to their families and friends, complete with a darkened meeting room and popcorn.

The love of exploring led Ansen through his Icarus period, a time as a teenager when he tried to fly. He bought an old parachute from an army supply store, fitted it with grommets and threaded those with bamboo poles placed at various angles. As I recall, this preparation took about a month, what with discussing his plans and stepping over that parachute dozens of times in the hallway to his room. One Saturday we were invited to come to a deserted field south of McAllen, one where there happened to be a small hill, and observe the culmination of Ansen's experiment. Ansen had rounded up assistants who now helped him lift the contraption into place, held various tie-down ropes, and one in particular who had a motorcycle. With the cycle revving, Ansen labored up the small incline (our only definition of a hill in this alluvial delta), gave the thumbs-up to his Evel Knievel, took off in tow, and eventually soared a few feet off the ground. Over and over they repeated the process, obviously hoping for more lift from the wind. He never did get close enough to the sun to melt, and we were glad. It was a fun morning, and we came home relieved, even happy, despite Leonardo's limited success. As I recall, he took the lesson in gravity in the way he accepted most things, with a touch of humor mixed with reality.

Ansen's close encounter with being airborne was the same year that Paul MacCready won the Kremer Prize of $100,000 for the first person who could achieve a mile-long, controlled, human-powered flight. His *Gossamer Condor* now hangs in the Smithsonian. Ansen at 16 was not as ready for such an accomplishment but it's interesting that he has throughout his career claimed the same activity that MacCready credits for much of his success: daydreaming.[3]

When Ansen was 17, he spent the summer with an Italian family on the island of Sardinia in the Mediterranean, thanks to a student exchange program headed up by local businessmen. Early one morning in June, we took him to catch the plane in Harlingen. As he sat in the back seat between his two brothers, I nervously admonished him about last-minute things. He was tolerating my anxiety with his usual "Okay, Mom" when we heard him say to his brothers in a soft dreamy voice, "Look at that sunrise!" We had surrendered him to a state of permanent wonder about the world around him.

This was to be his first airplane trip, incredible by today's standards, but it was 1978 and we were a no-frills family. That day there were seven tornadoes across the country and he arrived in New York in the evening much wiser about air travel.

He came home with many beautiful photos of the exotic island setting, along with pictures of common cats, chairs casting long shadows, and bougainvillea on walls. We teased him about going halfway around the world to take pictures of house cats, chairs, and a plant that also grew in his own backyard. The deeper meaning was that he had begun to practice his art, capturing with considerable attention and courage what he personally saw as most interesting, with a predilection for choosing objects and animals rather than people as his subjects.

Ansen comments that as a teen he thought he might be

"discovered" for some extraordinary talent. With years of work behind him, he reflects that "the 'discovery' by the outside world only comes from lots and lots of practice (and a little luck)." He quotes Louis Pasteur: "Chance favors the prepared mind," avowing that this is true for creativity as well. College at Trinity University in San Antonio found him shaping his own specialty in photography with the mentoring of a caring artist/professor. He soon found a part-time job at a photo studio and worked there throughout his college days.

Graduating in 1982 with a double major in art and communications, he stayed on in San Antonio in full-time work in photography, first for others and then establishing his own company.

In 1984, he had saved enough to buy a touring bicycle and explore Europe alone in the summer. We drove up to San Antonio to see him off. In my journal, I recorded this little conversation the night before he left:

Ansen: If anything happens to me, I don't want you and Dad to feel guilty. I don't want you to feel like you shouldn't have let me go.

Me: I didn't know we had that option! But I feel that if anything happens to you, you will have lived 23 very full years.

Ansen: That's right!

Me: Which is not to say 'Tempt fate.'

Ansen: No. There's a difference.

Once back home in San Antonio, while entertaining young foreigners who were working there, he met a young German nanny, whom he married in 1988. Doerte Weber is a master weaver, working with various textiles and active in the San Antonio arts community. In 1990, they had a son, Luca, and in 2013, Luca graduated from the University of Sterling in Scotland with a double major in (surprise for the Seales!) sports science and psychology.

Ansen feels his interest and participation in art came about principally from his environment and from his strong will power and determination. Reflecting on his childhood, he names some of the cogent factors in his shaping: The Make-it Drawer (see elsewhere), the orchard where our house was located outside McAllen, and "free time to be bored." His theory is that creativity comes from boredom, that is, the excess potential that the brain is trying to use.

Here I must interpose an early memory of Ansen and boredom. When he was in first grade in Denton, we got a note from his teacher asking us to come in for a conference; it seems things weren't going so well. She told us that Ansen was daydreaming too much, looking out the window, not knuckling down to classroom assignments. In a word, he was under-achieving. When we confronted him with this, he said, "We have too many mimeographed chickens to color. I don't like to color chickens." We got that straightened out so that he had more interesting things to do.

A Halloween note written by Ansen as a third grader says, "I want to be a pirait [pirate] and that is all. and theres NOTHING that can STOP ME, not enything at all." He commented recently that tasks requiring discipline in childhood helped prepare him for later, when he would need to concentrate to see an artistic project, however difficult, to conclusion. As a boy, he mowed the yard, copied musical score parts for his dad, practiced the piano and trombone, and performed in choirs and operas—activities requiring attention and follow-through. Additionally, as is usual with the firstborn, Ansen undoubtedly got a heavy dose of parental expectation and guidance as we worked our way through the new experience. For better or worse, we demanded a lot of him.

The age-old artist's dilemma of how to practice one's art and also put bread on the table seems to have been resolved in Ansen's life. "I used to apologize for having to make a living shooting pillows, perfume, pet food and anything else somebody wanted to sell. I really just wanted people to know me as an artist. But I now realize that every commercial shoot I do helps me hone my skills and that I couldn't do the art as well without that experience."

Ansen feels his participation in art as fulfilling an obligation willingly, one of gratitude for having been given, and earning, the talents and skills that he is now using. "I also get strength to carry on by knowing that I'm part of a long tradition, and that I may be able to help others continue that tradition through teaching and sharing what I know."

Ansen wryly proclaims himself "a novelty junkie" with a need to move forward always in his art-making with new subjects, media, and techniques. In his thirty years of work in the field of art photography, he has explored black-and-white images, specialized in photographing other artists' works including archeological artifacts in Tuscany, developed a portfolio of animal images, and served as official photographer for both the Mutual UFO Network and the Rock Art Foundation of Texas.

More recently, he has explored global cultural symbols, sacred texts, and mathematical symbols in a series called "Bloodlines," investigated in Germany the translation of photographic images into stained glass, traveled to China and the Canary Islands in cultural arts exchange programs, and used giant images with imbedded LED lighting for commissioned public art.

Ansen's creativity often branches out into science, math, and technology. He recalls being impressed with his paternal grandfather's patience and ability to make special tools he needed in order to complete a wooden craft piece he was working on. Times and tools have changed but Ansen follows his Pop's example by creating special custom attachments and programs for his robotic router. This machine cuts pointillistic holes into clear acrylic to achieve Ansen's giant photo/sculptures.

"The process of producing the art is what keeps me interested; always different, always changing," he says. "In this way, I was born at just the right time to catch the wave of the digital revolution and to be able to grow and change with it."

Erren: Graphic Design and Cultural Arts

When Erren was 12, I asked him to draw a Santa. He said Sure, grabbed pen and paper, and began. I watched as he started in the lower right corner of the paper with Santa's right foot. But instead of drawing the other foot and proceeding symmetrically with both legs, both arms, et cetera, he continued to draw up one side, with one arm, then the head with face, and down the other side. When he finished there was a cute little cartoon Santa, with all his limbs equal. The figure was the right size to fill up the space on the page and to allow for the details of face and costume that Erren added.

I asked Erren how he could just start on the page in a certain place and go directly to the rest of the image without planning and drawing the figure with parallel parts. He said, "Oh, that's easy. First I see all of it in my mind and then just fill it in on the page."

This unique way of seeing his world reflects his abilities in artistic design, which have served him so far in his life in a number of endeavors. After he graduated from the University of Texas at Austin with a Bachelor of Fine Arts, Erren worked as a production artist for an advertising firm in Austin for a year. Pursuing his dream to live near the beach, he moved to the South Padre Island area and worked for a few months as jewelry manager for an upscale Valley retail firm. In 1986, he moved back to McAllen and freelanced for several small ad agencies, while gradually gaining his own clients for graphic design and ad copy. In 1992, as visual arts technology was changing almost daily, he went to Houston to study computer graphic design—applying for a job that used the skills he wanted, watching those around him, and learning the discipline while making a living. After a few months of working for a package design firm whose clients included Minute Maid and Imperial Sugar, he returned to the Valley and resumed his advertising design and copy writing business with renewed vigor.

Over the next five years, he enjoyed growing a brisk practice, with clients in economic development, tourism, retail, finance, real estate, health care, non-profit businesses and other fields. He garnered many local advertising awards and a handful of regional and national honors. But these successes in the frantic world of advertising made impossible demands on his desire to manage the ever-increasing aspects of his work. (Micro-managing crops up in all the Seales' creative efforts. Note that same trait in Ansen's photographic practice, where he likes "to control the artistic process from start to finish.") Practically, Erren needed a much larger studio and staff to support his client base. Realizing that he had an aversion to expansion, he gradually and rather painfully, both for him and his satisfied clients, phased out his one-person advertising firm.

Reflecting on his needs—"I do need beauty (mostly visual) in my life and an aesthetic challenge most of the time"—he decided to open an antiques and cultural arts store with his partner Fernando Rivera, originally a biochemical engineer from Torreon, Mexico.

Starting small in 1998, they stocked their first store with auction-bought antiques, books, and decorative objects. Today, in their second location, a large old warehouse of about 5,000 square feet located at a busy intersection in McAllen, VIDA has a faithful clientele and a brisk walk-in trade. Large furniture, old doors, and architectural pieces imported from Mexico, India, and China are interspersed with candles, pillows, crosses, jewelry, incense, flowers, and wall decor.

With a desire to do their part to preserve an historic enclave of houses near downtown McAllen, he and Fernando, putting talent and equity to work, have bought and restored four older houses, including their residence, a two-story 1929 Pueblo-style home built by a McAllen pioneer.

Very early on, Erren began rearranging, modifying, and decorating anything around. As a child, his hands were constantly busy— fidgeting, molding, reshaping, re-combining any objects within reach. Once, in a fit of motherly exasperation I said to him, "Erren, stop! Just let your hands be still!" As I recall, he was obsessively re-inventing uses for a bright strip of ribbon. He replied, "But Mom, I'm just doing this to keep from going crazy." I never again reprimanded him...at least for that.

The McAllen International Museum offered art lessons for youngsters and both Erren and Avrel took advantage of these for a couple of years. They had excellent guidance under the tutelage of Sue

Robertson, a local commercial artist, so much so that Erren claims Robertson as one of his career role models.

Erren labels his early artist self-image as "creative arrogance." "I knew I could always come up with the best (or one of the best) ideas for art projects or skits or the like. Since I was so lousy at sports and competitive activities, art and performing—things at which I could excel—garnered praise from teachers and classmates. And all creative people love that kind of attention, especially those who say they don't!"

Erren remembers that the closest he felt to failure in high school was when he did not make the cut playing French horn to be in the All Region Band after winning a seat the previous year. However, he makes the distinction, and I think it is an important one, that playing the French horn was not necessarily creative, but rather an artistic skill. He labels the try-out as "a technical exhibition—it had none of the endorphins that real creativity produces, mainly just fear."

In his early teens, he decorated family birthday and anniversary cakes and painted the entire walls and ceiling of his bedroom as a jungle, replete with vines, palm trees, and flowers.

In high school, he designed tee shirts and made posters for school organization events. One day in class he saucily cartooned two of his American Studies teachers who team-taught. Mrs. B was glamorous, with long beautiful hair, a full bosom, and high heels. Mrs. G, much shorter, was depicted as neatly coiffed, with comfortable shoes, twirling her pearl strands. The story goes that the picture was being passed around when it got the attention of Mrs. B, who, in an act of discipline, confiscated it, took one look, and howled with laughter. She showed it to Mrs. G, and they made copies and merrily put them up in the teachers' lounge. Soon, the whole faculty was laughing with them. A year later, when Erren graduated, we had the images put on tee shirts and gave them as gifts to these long-suffering wonderful teachers.

Growing up, Erren was interested in drama and performed in a number of plays. After college, he sang the part of Seymour, the male lead in a Valley production of *Little Shop of Horrors*. One interesting set of roles he played was the child's lead in his father's opera *The Atonement* in 1975, at age 12, and the role of the raging adult simpleton in the same opera, at 37, in its 25th anniversary production in 2000.

When Erren was 13, he was fitted with a Milwaukee brace, a contraption of steel bars, fiberglass, and leather from chin to hips for the treatment of scoliosis. The pediatric orthopedist helpfully described it as "a real birdcage, something out of the Inquisition." This brace corrects spinal curvature during the rapid adolescent growing period. Erren entered treatment at Thanksgiving of the seventh grade and finished in January of his junior year in high school, the first three years wearing the brace 23 hours a day.

Going into baggy men's clothes and being held rigidly from hips to head was not an easy thing for a thirteen year old. But from the beginning, Erren was able to verbalize his situation. The first night he slept in it, he said as he headed for bed, "Well, I guess I'll go meet it face to brace."

Here is my poem about the subject:

To a son, in a steel body brace

Today, visiting a garden, I saw a sparrow cage,
a sturdy box with a trap door where,
when the sparrows come to eat,
they fall and are caught.
The two in it were thrashing about,
unable to understand the meaning of wire.

I thought of you,
walking around with a cage hooked to you,
your arms and legs sticking out, wing and claw,

how you cried and thrashed about
that first night
and I unable to help
on the floor by your bed.[1]

During those years, he cultivated friendships, especially in the band, where he played French horn and marched at all the games, and in his youth group at church, where he participated in programs, dramas, and camp. What he was limited in doing physically, he made up for with energy, sharp wit, and an indomitable talent for partying. During his junior high years, if we forgot a party he was supposed to attend, we would get a phone call: "Is Erren coming? We're waiting to start until he gets here."

In an account of family creativity, I mention this period in Erren's life because, in a peculiar and certainly not intentional way, wearing the brace probably accelerated his will power and certainly enhanced his coping skills. At an age of peak herd instinct, with social communing and physical acceptability foremost in teens' minds, Erren had to invent his individual way. The brace both stilled and liberated him—to think, plan, and invent things to do "to keep from going crazy."

Today, Erren continues to explore creative possibilities, both in his work as a retail merchant and privately as an artist. "I probably chose my current art forms for two reasons: economic viability (things that make money—graphic design, illustration) and things that come easily and are fun (interior design, buying, creating a 'look' by assembling items, visual merchandising). Now that I'm painting and searching for challenges, that is changing somewhat. I'm trying to jump-start that 'soul-filling' feeling that I get when creativity is really flowing. Sometimes I get it gardening, or painting, or decorating for Christmas. It's that pure fun feeling when you're making something out of nothing. It's just coming out of you with no resistance."

Of the store, he comments, "I think there is artistry in store display, in buying artfully, in flower arranging, in interior design, in advertising for the store, in designing the store interior." Perhaps, he muses, this is not the same pure "fine art" that most artists want, but it is better than having a job that does not involve art at all.

After establishing himself in commerce and community activities, first through his graphic design business and then in his unique store VIDA, Erren is beginning, as he approaches midlife, to have the time for exploring the personal side of art, as he puts it, "dreaming about creativity without time constraints or monetary payoff." In recent times, his travels in Europe, Australia, South America, and India have expanded his love of cultural arts.

Through the years, Erren has experimented with watercolor, oil painting, and craft-based art. Although he has not done any ceramics since he finished a course in college, a few pitchers and bowls from that time are still around. His final project for that class might serve to illustrate Erren's whimsical approach to art.

When others in the class chose substantial philosophical artist statements as their final class project, Erren chose for his subject "How

Bacon Is Made." In a free-standing set of ceramic scenes, a business pig in tie with briefcase de-planes in the tropics. Next, the pig, replete with koozie and sunshades, spreads his blanket on the beach and begins his tanning. The final scenes show the pig gradually losing form, in the end becoming a crisp strip of bacon on the pallet. From vacation to bacon-ation.

In a personal appraisal, Erren comments, "For me art is not like water, in that you can't live a day without it. It's more like vitamins: go without for a long time and you feel deficient. Sometimes it's like alcohol: it's fun to be drunk on it now and then. It makes life more bearable." He realizes that "Art is a cultural necessity" but for him, it is "an individual luxury."

Avrel: Writing and Music

When Avrel was nine, he wrote a letter to his grandparents containing this message: "I want to tell you about my victory in the newspaper. I sent in a picture for them to publish and they did!" He enclosed a copy of it, a rather nice proportional line drawing of a camel in the desert. Little did any of us know that his "victory in the newspaper" would manifest itself in a career in journalism, editing, and writing.

For 17 years he was editor of *The Alcalde,* The University of Texas at Austin alumni magazine. In that role, he had occasion to interview and write about many of The University of Texas' prominent alumni, such as journalists Bill Moyers and Catherine Crier, U.S. Secretary of the Treasury Lloyd Bentsen, NFL hall of famer Earl Campbell, and Alan Bean, the fourth man on the moon. Another exciting avenue of contact was Avrel's interviews with the academic stars of the faculty and staff, including Nobel laureate Ilya Prigogine, conservative social critic Marvin Olasky, and five University of Texas presidents.

After a brief interval of work in the corporate world, Avrel was selected in 2010 as the speech writer for the president of The University of Texas at Austin, a position he presently holds with enthusiasm and the expertise of one who had already studied for many years the university atmosphere.

The books Avrel has authored have been an anchor for his fertile mind and heart, and a source of pleasure to friends and family. *The Hull, the Sail, and the Rudder* is a philosophical memoir of his growing up. *Dude: A Generation X Memoir* celebrates all the meanings of the title. *The Tree: A Spiritual Proposition* suggests the tree as a natural reflection of a spiritual premise. *The Messengers*, a children's book, takes the young reader through parallel elements of several major faiths. *True Freedom and the Wisdom of Virtue* discusses the Bahá'í religion's principles of personal morality. *The Secret of Suranesh* portrays the allegorical journey of a young man seeking the meaning of life. In 2005, Avrel wrote, filmed, and produced, along with his friend Jay Galvan, an independent film of the Suranesh story. (See the appendix for his account of this.)

From the time he was participating in a very active program of communications classes at Memorial High School in McAllen, Avrel wanted to be a broadcast "on-camera" reporter. While he was still in high school, he became a radio announcer for high school football games and acquired a job on the weekends deejaying at a local radio station.

In the spring of 1989 Avrel graduated from The University of Texas at Austin with a bachelor of arts degree in radio-TV-film. He had in hand the requisite demonstration video and recommendations from his professors to begin making the rounds of TV stations.

But he soon learned that 1989 was not the year for hiring an inexperienced young Anglo male seeking a TV position. He came home to McAllen (in today's parlance, a boomerang kid) and, continuing his quest, took jobs to make ends meet—a temp in a business office and a substitute teacher. One day he found himself applying for a job as a reporter for the local daily, *The Monitor*. After all, it was words and ideas, and maybe it would be a stepping stone to a television job.

Frankly, I was astounded when he came home with the news he'd been hired to gather news. It wouldn't last long. As a small child, Avrel exasperated me by winding himself in my skirt in order to hide from someone when I was trying to get him to say hello. And although he had later proven himself in public speaking by his part-time radio jobs and training at the university, as well as fronting his high school rock band THE PLAN (more on this later), these things had not required personal interaction. Avrel was a curious blend of social wariness, even diffi-dence, and entertainment art. So, how was he going to get up the nerve to go out and do a cold interview? Took after his dad's side. Reserved.

Furthermore, Avrel had resisted all my attempts to get him to enlarge on his ability to write. He had showed me a few of his essays and I was truly impressed with his wit for light subjects and his depth on weightier ones. I had urged him to send these out to a few magazines on speculation. Nah, he didn't think he'd be interested in doing that. (My own observation: A mother's opinion is scarily powerful, both positive and negative, and is often the first to be rejected.)

Yes, he had written plays with a like-minded friend as they were growing up, spending hours acting them out, as well as staging *Planet of the Apes*, *Star Wars,* and *Jesus Christ Superstar* in garages, back-yards, and vacant lots. And he'd even written a book in the eighth grade, *The Three Fires*, a sequel to C.S. Lewis's *Narnia* series, because, he explained, he was too disappointed that there were only seven of those stories. He typed the book and we "published" it at the local copy store and bound a few copies with a spiral binding. His friend David wrote in the prologue that "the quality of Seale's writings could well issue in another great decade in epic fantasy!" Okay, they were thirteen and the world was theirs.

There are times when Providence furnishes ways to keep parents humble. Not only did the young adult prove himself at the newspaper in routine office assignments, but he jumped over fences, knocked on doors, glad-handed folks, and presented smashing story ideas at staff meetings. In a couple of months, he announced that he had become a humor columnist for the paper, and after a few weeks of that, he proposed and had accepted a twice-weekly expanded column of commentary on local and national issues dubbed "Culturewatch." He wrote with authority and zest on such things as odious TV commercials, Elvis memorabilia, ad slogans, politically correct ideas, the Grammys, traffic stress, ugly street signs, country living, and manual labor. All this sparkling commentary quickly earned him an admiring audience in the community.

After two years at *The Monitor,* the siren call of Austin came. Gone were the application videos for on-camera weather and news reporting. He secured a position as assistant editor for *The Alcalde,* the University of Texas bi-monthly alumni magazine. Another year saw the long-time editor retiring, and Avrel, ever-surprising, thought he was up to it, applied for, and became the interim editor. Another year brought the full senior editorship, a permanent position he held for another fifteen years.

During that time, he met and married Kirstin Books, a graduate of The University of Texas with a degree in French. The two of them have replicated his birth family. They are raising three sons, Andrew, Cameron, and Ian.

When Avrel was about to graduate from high school, we sent him to the Johnson O'Connor testing laboratory in Houston to help him discover what he was suited for. One of their conclusions was that whatever profession he chose, he should always have music in his life. He wouldn't be happy or balanced without it. He was by this time playing with various degrees of ease the violin, guitar, and piano, as well as singing in choirs.

Early on, Avrel took to the piano readily and worked especially hard to earn little plaster busts of composers his teacher gave as reward for completed work (which, by the way, he is now passing down to his own children). After a brief period of formal piano lessons, Avrel continued to play, improvising and figuring out tunes he heard and liked. He started to play the guitar with an enthusiasm that he lacked for violin, though he continued violin lessons as a young teen and played throughout high school in his father's Valley Symphony Orchestra.

In high school he formed a rock band with a couple of his friends and this endeavor took up most of their free time—practicing, getting gigs, messing with their equipment, making stage props, and planning their grunge-wear. Gratefully, they were allowed by one of the benevolent parents to practice after-hours in his retail store. We actually never encouraged Avrel with THE PLAN, but neither did we discourage him. We were mostly concerned about the deafening effect of the high decibels on the boys' hearing, the lifestyle of famous rockers which the boys might try to imitate, and the respectability of the places where they played. We hoped and prayed that Avrel wouldn't make a career of it.

Meanwhile, he practiced hours and hours on his guitar, with his own method of learning new songs: listening to professional guitarists on tape and copying what they did. Although he could read musical scores, he didn't care to learn that way. He'd rather listen, and then just *do* it. It was a method of music-making that his dad and I were not adept in, and although we didn't care for the rock music, we marveled at his ability to play by ear.

His brothers had chosen to be in their high school's symphonic and marching bands, but Avrel chose to sing in the choir. He was a valuable *basso profundo* (the lowest bass) appreciated by his teachers, and he didn't have to march at football games. Besides, he was already playing instruments—piano, violin, and guitar—which did not fit into school band instrumentation.

During college, Avrel and his friends would reconstitute their band during the summer and winter breaks, and upon graduating and moving back to the Valley, they began playing professionally for the first time, with a brief but busy period of performing in South Texas night clubs. When the band members eventually took full-time jobs in far-flung cities, Avrel's focus shifted to solo acoustic guitar, learning solo-acoustic repertoire and arranging and his own instrumental versions of pop, folk, and classical standards. He continues playing to this day, much to the delight of his family and friends. He plays occasionally at coffee houses and for weddings, work parties, and other social occasions. And 25 years on, he has married these two strands, some-times reuniting with his old band mates and resurrecting their pop set but with him on acoustic guitar.

There is a strong component in Avrel's life and art of spiritual questing. Five of the eight books he has authored speak both directly and indirectly to matters of spirituality. In his pocket-sized book titled *True Freedom*, he notes the ultimate source of his creative bent: "At day's end, we are only able to achieve intellectually if we have the right hardware, if our neural architecture is sound and our biochemistry is stable. And who can claim credit for that? It is common to think of ourselves as 'co-creators' of our lives. And that is true to a large degree. But when you compare the part that you have created to the part that God has created, the only response can be one of utter humility and extreme modesty about one's own accomplishments..."[1]

Avrel is a disciple of the Bahá'í world faith and feels, as believers in most world religions, the tension between service and ego. He puts it this way: "These are dicey waters I have had to navigate...It requires constant vigilance to ensure that my motives are as pure as they can be, and that the artistic 'calling' doesn't begin to poison the spiritual 'calling' with elements of ego."

Avrel is an involved family man, particularly relishing making music with his sons, taking them camping, building things together, and dad-coaching their sports. Beyond all this, he steals moments to write. In the vein of the proverbial busman's holiday, Avrel works on his next book on the way to work—a writing job—in the park-and-ride shuttle he takes to the U.T. campus from Austin's far north side.

One major tendency in Avrel's work is, by his own words, "driven by a compulsion to define, categorize, and through those, to surmise the biggest possible picture of the universe—always to 'zoom out,' in cinematic terms. The synthesis of this fluency drives my creativity." This explains his predilection to tackle big subjects in his books: personal evolution of body, mind, and soul; all the iterations of the term "Dude"; the essence of morality; and a youth's quest for meaning.

Daniel Coyle in *The Talent Code* writes that some people are "purposely operating at the edge of their ability."[2] Another of Avrel's tendencies is to take whatever he's interested in a step further. "This business of its having to be my discovery is something that I have only recently put my finger on. I'm only able to really give myself over to something completely if it is my discovery, or at least if *I think* it is my discovery. I am stubborn and egocentric in this way."

Avrel's eclectic tastes and multi-faceted avenues of creativity stem, of course, from his unique personality. He estimates that his psycho-spiritual need accounts for about sixty percent of his reason for pursuing his art. He says the word that comes to him, when he thinks of creativity, is "fulfillment." He defines this, as "the sensation that you are doing that which you have been put on the earth to do.... I default to doing what I do. I don't consider it virtuous; I simply see it as answering a constant thirst. I believe we are happy to the degree that we are responding to and fulfilling our calling in life."

He feels that his art is something he does primarily because "it is something I cannot keep from doing."

Carl: Musical Passion and Mission

Carl had a whimsical memory of himself as a little guy of about eight experimenting with music. In his home a tobacco stand stood beside his father's chair, just a box with a couple of drawers balanced on turned legs. Carl would take that as his music stand, and with a pencil for a conductor's baton, he practiced conducting. Where did the music come from? The radio, and sometimes he just made it up and sang as he went along. Here was a combination of his life work, conducting and composing, expressing itself early on.

Carl's family moved from Ft. Worth to the Rio Grande Valley when he was 15, settling in the small town of La Feria. Carl was already playing the saxophone, a family heirloom that his mother had played in vaudeville.

Determined to major in music and become a band director, Carl first went to college at North Texas State University, then switched to Baylor and quickly became a leader among the students of the music school, and literally so as the drum major of the Baylor Golden Wave Band. He played oboe in the Baylor Symphony and became proficient in flute and bassoon, as well as knowledgeable about the other instruments in band and orchestra. He took his bachelor of music degree in August,1958 and, our having married in April, we launched ourselves off to Kentucky, where he had a fellowship to be the marching band director of the University of Louisville Cardinal Band while he obtained his master's degree in music.

After two happy years in Kentucky, he and I returned to Texas. Vainly searching for a band director's job in the Rio Grande Valley, he accepted a position as the orchestra director for the Edinburg Independent School District string program. The next year, he became the director of the band program for the Harlingen school district. It took him six years to decide that the job's emphasis on football games and parades was not his calling. As Joseph Campbell said, "You must give up the life you planned in order to have the life that is waiting for you."[1]

So in 1967, we moved to Denton with our three young sons where he enrolled in the music school at North Texas State University and four years later received his Doctor of Musical Arts in Music Composition.

We returned to the Valley and after a year of substitute teaching, a position for Carl opened up at Pan American University teaching in the music department. Very shortly, the conductorship of the Pan American Orchestra became available and Carl moved into it, eager to increase enrollment and schedule more concerts for an expanding audience.

In those early days, Carl did almost every job associated with the symphony. For one class-load teaching credit, he chose the repertoire, ordered the music, scheduled concerts, auditioned members, sorted and distributed the music, dealt with the widely variant tastes of concert-goers, arranged chairs and stands, and, on occasion, even drove the instrument truck. These duties were in addition to weekly rehearsals and a concert season of four to six concerts.

From the beginning, the university and the wider Valley community had cooperated to make the orchestra viable. The university provided a conductor through its music department, a physical home for the orchestra, gave class credit to the few students who were enrolled as players, and supplied the music and several of the more expensive instruments. Under Carl's leadership, the Pan American Orchestra evolved into the Valley Symphony Orchestra, with a supporting South Texas Symphony Association.

Throughout his career as orchestra conductor, Carl maintained an active teaching schedule at the university. His specialties were music theory, orchestration, form and analysis, and teaching private lessons on the oboe and bassoon.

As if to underscore the "Never say never" mantra, Carl recalled a music class in his sixth grade:

"Something I did not like was a sixth grade class in music appreciation where the teacher had us hold one hand as if it were a music staff of five lines and four spaces and with our other hand make like we knew how to identify pitches of songs by pointing to the place on the 'staff.' I clearly remember thinking 'What is this all about?' I think the music teacher had only one lesson plan, because I remember multiple repetitions of listening to Grieg's 'In the Hall of the Mountain King.'"

For six years, he acted as Music Department head. During this time he gave up his position as choir director at the First Presbyterian Church of McAllen, eventually returning to the post for a few years, for a total of 24 years as the church's choirmaster.

In the 1980's, Carl was appointed by Governor Dolph Briscoe to the Good Neighbor Commission. Carl became interested in touring in Mexico, and with the help of the Mexican government, the Valley Symphony Orchestra was able to take several tours into the neighboring states of Nuevo Leon and Tamaulipas. He also guest-conducted orchestras in Guanajuato, Tampico, Salamanca, Morelia, Leon, Saltillo, and Monterrey.

So his life was built around music: conducting, composing, teaching, playing, and singing it. Carl commented about these years, "I have been lucky in that my job has also been my art. I have always felt, when involved in a music project, whether composing or producing music, that I was doing what I was being paid to do. So I felt free to 'hide' my 'fun' activities under the umbrella of 'job' without guilt. Placing a label on my music-related art, I would say that mission and passion share equal positions."

At 78, he said of his life and work, "If I had a mission statement—which I've never considered—it would contain words like fun, satisfaction, meaning, growth, fulfillment, sharing, new, and complete."

Carl reminisced about this mysterious art of music which he had given his life to: "Sound; the ephemeral is the eternal; beyond words; music is nonsense, in the sense of 'makes no word sense' and thus is perhaps the greatest sense of all, because it goes for the soul, the heart, and is untranslatable, the place beyond poetry where the human spirit can visit."

Jan: Writing and Teaching

I can remember a certain moment in my early childhood when I put a book of poetry down and said, "I can do that." I had just read a bird poem which tickled my mind and ears. It did not feel like a foreign object. I took it into myself and made the process mine, reached for my Big Chief tablet and pencil and went to work on a poem of my own.

Someone has said that it isn't mandatory in order to be a writer to have had a bad childhood, but it helps. Mine was not bad, just different. I was sickly as a child and spent most of my time alone. In a curious way, sitting alone in bed for two years when I was five and six on bed rest for tuberculosis probably contributed to my career in writing. In those years I learned to use my mind independent of everyone and everything around me. My chief entertainment was my thoughts.

By the time I was allowed to go to school regularly, in the latter half of the second grade, I was already practicing a secret mental life. I could read very well, I had memorized poems on my own, and I had begun that lifelong dialogue with one's self that is the torture and boon of writers. As a freshman at Baylor, I won a quatrain contest, the prize being a book of poetry by the 1956 Texas Poet Laureate. Hmmm, I thought, this is nice, but what's a poet laureate? Fifty-five years later I was to get a rather full definition by being named the 2012 Texas Poet Laureate.

I started playing the flute when I was eleven. When my parents saw that I would probably stay with it through adulthood, they sacrificed and bought me a professional Haynes model. I quickly grew to love it and it's been like a friend through all these years of playing, first on scholarship in college and then for church and special occasions.

Halfway through Baylor, I married Carl and we moved to Louisville, Kentucky, where I took all my elective hours in creative writing workshops. After graduating with a bachelor's degree in English from the University of Louisville, I continued to write poems but began to make use of my writing training in a completely different way.

Pregnant with Ansen when I graduated, I ended up in South Texas with a baby, a husband on a ridiculously low teacher's salary, and the need to generate some funds while I rocked the cradle. I discovered that I could write articles of common sense about baby care, sell them to parenting magazines, and get ready cash.

In Harlingen, I finally got to exercise my Texas teacher's certificate by teaching high school English for a couple of years, one before the birth of Erren and one before Avrel's appearance.

Earlier in this book I touch on our time in graduate school at North Texas State University with three little ones. In the four years we spent there, I finished a master's in English and taught for a year as a fulltime instructor in the English department.

The way I wanted to "do" motherhood was very time-costly but so is writing and needing to bring in income for the family. Still, I don't think I ever felt the boys were an imposition. Rather, they were a joy and a source of subjects for exploration in my writing. The subject matter of one of my books, *Sharing the House*, is about being a parent. Short stories that gained wide audiences in big-city newspapers in the '90s, such as " The Past Tense of Mom," "Reluctant Madonna" and "Jack of Hearts"[1] emanated from this primal relationship.

When we returned to the Valley from graduate school, I took a job for one year at North Junior High in Edinburg and then got on the faculty at Pan American University teaching English. Ten years later and after teaching 17 different courses at Pan American, I was awarded a poetry fellowship through the National Endowment of the Arts which allowed me to go on sabbatical for a year in 1982. After that, I taught two more years; then, bitten by the possibility of writing more, as well as suffering from a chronic illness, I resigned.

Being home a couple of years and in better health after two surgeries at the Mayo Clinic, I began to miss teaching, so I created a little cottage industry for myself by fashioning short-term classes in memoir and creative writing at the Hidalgo County Historical Museum in Edinburg, an arrangement which prevailed for twenty years.

When I look back on my writing life, I am rather shocked that it has lasted some 65 years, through childhood and teen years, the birth and raising of three children, a long marriage to a man in the public eye, a chronic illness, twelve relocations, and—hundreds of rejection slips.

One is one's own worst analyst so I can only guess at why I have kept on keeping on.

But out of those years have come nine books of poetry, collections of short stories and essays, a textbook on memoir writing, a biography, and several children's books.

The way I see it, there are positions to be filled in any civilization, from plumbers to priests. I happen to be stationed in the writers' position. This is simply my karmic assignment. I write because, deep inside, there's an implant for writing. If I did not write, I would be unhappy. In the times in my life when I have been barred by circumstance from writing, I have become depressed. So whether things are going well or poorly, I know that eventually I have to get back to the words.

I have never lacked for subjects to write about. I'm with Robert Louis Stevenson who wrote, "The world is so full of a number of things/ I'm sure we should all be as happy as kings."[2] Hardly a day goes by that I don't notice something that I think could be used in a piece of writing. My propensity for close observation has led me to write in different genres.

Recently my life took a sharp turn. Just as I was beginning to settle into a gentle stay-at-home, read-the-paper-and-cook-supper retirement routine, I was appointed Texas Poet Laureate for 2012 by the Texas Legislature, a position I will retain for life. Although there are no specific duties, many publishing and speaking opportunities occurred during the year. Three books received publication during that time. I travelled 26,000 miles in Texas, making 117 presentations in colleges, public schools, clubs, churches, associations, and teachers' groups. I surmise that I may continue doing at least some of these things for the rest of my active life. The honor is far more than I ever dreamed of, coming near the end of a life that I am profoundly thankful for in all its variety.

Part Four: The Home as Lab

Introduction

During the years of this project, I have gone to Ansen, Erren, and Avrel with various questions on their perceptions of growing up as they did. I have also sought out their answers from their writing in magazines, on blogs, and in letters. Here are their observations, as well as Carl's and mine.

Free Time and the Make-It Drawer

A British television program titled *Child of Our Time: Killing Creativity* adapted the work of author Norman Jackson in his observations that unstructured play develops problem-solving, self-monitoring, and the control of emotions and behavior. He laments the increase in our times of "adult-led toy-centered rule-bound play" and names two types of play which limit creativity: 1) sanitized play, as in "Don't get dirty" and 2) play with greatly manufactured toys.[1]

True, but there's something to be said for open-ended toys. In one of my letters home, I write, "The boys loved their flashlights. We have already gotten new 'bladders' [batteries] for them. They have investigated every nook and cranny in this house and Ansen wants to pull all the curtains drawn so it will be dark and their lights will show up better." I go on to request toys for their Christmas because "toys are things we seldom can let go of the money for." From this distance, not a bad thing.

Okay, so flashlights were manufactured toys, but only slightly, and they promoted open-ended play. In my journal in a category called "Impossible Projects," (besides the paper and tape projects of an earlier essay, and Avrel's rock collection pasted on notebook paper), there are listings of playhouses out of encyclopedia volumes, fish in vitamin bottles, a terrarium of Johnson grass, and a farm in a cardboard box.

All three boys recall vast stretches of free play. Avrel remembers "Saturdays and eternal summer days, in which we could just play and play and play, and creativity inevitably rushed in to fill the void...It's in those times that imagination is really stretched."

When Ansen was a toddler, I wrote in a letter to my parents, "If I want to rest, he goes off in his room to play or stays outside playing with the puppy." Ansen has a major theory that works for him: boredom breeds creativity, boredom being "the excess potential of the human brain." He noted that he "always found lots of ideas in the orchard; wandering and pondering." He acknowledged that the free time was interspersed with "frantic times of intense intellectual stimulation at school...but the quiet times were the impetus to *act* on the information gathered in the frantic times."

Earlier in this book I wrote about our life in an orchard in "The Pursuit of Happiness." We returned to the Valley from graduate school with three children, two more degrees, and $700. We settled in an old farmhouse north of McAllen which sat in forty acres of orange and grapefruit trees. There was also a drainage ditch, an orchard dog, an orchard guinea hen, a mulberry tree house, and a single hidden tangerine tree, prized by the boys for its super-sweet fruit. It was our experiment in roughing it. The boys often speak of those three years as the favorites of their childhoods. Those years were some of the best "free time" years.

When we lived in the orchard, our dachshund Taffy was gotten to by Creep, the sheep dog that came with the old house. In my journal, I make this notation: "Taffy—4 large puppies delivered Caesarian. Vet said he could have used forceps but they would all be born dead. We opted for $40 hound dogs—not really a very expensive toy for 3 boys nowadays."

All three sons listed "The Make-It Drawer" as a powerful influence. This was a large drawer, usually in a bathroom, into which we placed all kinds of left-over materials such as odd buttons, old watches, broken jewelry, used computer paper, broken thingamajigs, bits of lace and ribbons, Styrofoam forms, broken crayons, used gift wrappings, bits of fabric, old socks, and burned-out light bulbs. The guys went to this drawer when they needed something to fill their time, or if they had an idea for making a puppet or drawing a picture.

Thinking back on that conglomerate, Erren commented, "I don't know that we ever maxed out the make-it drawer, but knowing it was there was always an inspiration—and 'no excuse to be bored.'" Avrel replied, "I remember having lots of stuff to draw on and write on—and things to noodle around with." He cited used accordion-folded computer paper and second sheets of copier paper that Carl and I saved and brought home to them from our teaching jobs.

The make-it drawer was a low-brow creativity kit, spawned out of the strained budget of two school teachers, at one time back in graduate school, at another building a house, all the while crazily writing poems and musical compositions. Years later, Avrel tactfully labeled our barely

middle-class existence of those years as "freedom from consumerism."
He continued, "Whereas my friends might come home with the latest
and greatest Mattel action figure of Darth Vader, the middle-class
exigencies of our household freed us from the sometimes constricting
pattern of having everything just *so*. That forced/allowed us to pursue
homemade options, like Darth Vader made from a Pringles can with a
painted light bulb ringed by a Spirograph template for the head."

Encouragement

In Avrel's book *True Freedom*, he writes, "Criticism has long superseded creation. If more people created, they would be less likely to criticize so freely."[1]

Maybe because Carl and I were artists and highly sensitive to negative criticism of our artistic endeavors, we as parents were naturally careful about any adverse remarks about the boys' creative efforts. Carl had plenty of turn-downs for proposed performances of his musical compositions, and I can attest to hundreds of rejection slips on my writing.

We not only refrained from critical remarks, but in fact were often delighted with their creations. Why would we want to put down an intriguing photograph, the decorations of a birthday cake, or a freehand drawing of George Washington?

It's only been in the last few years that I've recognized what playful parents are often doing when they go all-out for their kids: they're reliving or filling in the blanks of their own childhood. We often gave our time and energy to their ideas. I sewed costumes for them: a red band uniform for little Ansen made out of red curtains (a la Scarlet?); a Dracula cape for Erren; a circus dog outfit (told about in "The Doggone First Grader") for Avrel; and a white bunny suit complete with pink stand-up wire ears.

We always had special themed birthday parties for them through their elementary years. One memorable one was a carnival theme for Erren's sixth birthday, complete with homemade rides and games managed by Carl and fortunes told by a costumed lady looking suspiciously like Erren's mother.

Their cakes were exclusively homemade, not entirely because I wanted to honor them with painstaking labor—although that was true—but also because we never had the money to buy one from the bakery.

As adult parents, Ansen and Avrel and their wives have continued the tradition. They've had space and cowboy and sports themes for their children, along with beautiful homemade cakes with more daring designs than I ever dreamed of putting together, things like soccer balls and guitars. One party featured a table-top *active* volcano cake.

Erren and his partner Fernando are famous for their clever parties for family and friends with fabulous decorations, food, and entertainment. Erren undoubtedly would be able to do this anyway but I like to think that a few of these talents stem from that long-ago tradition in our family.

Elsewhere in the book are examples of ways we played together as a family—not really in any special way, just quite ordinarily as millions of other families do.

When Ansen was asked about being encouraged, he replied, "I always felt that you, Mom and Dad, were very supportive of what I produced. I could always count on you to give lots of compliments. You and Dad always encouraged us to be different, do things in different ways...at least that's what I thought you wanted from us. I especially remember Dad saying this. It may not have been a recurring theme in our conversations. It may have just been one or two particularly well-timed suggestions. But for some reason, I think of this as the main theme of our interactions regarding anything creative. 'If you can't do it differently from everybody else, it's not worth doing.'"

In this regard, I have to add that long since Ansen picked up on this, we find that "original" or "re-imagining" is one of the four areas of intellectual activity named for testing in school programs.

Erren was very confident of his "creations," as he dubbed them. "I think I was steeled against criticism. I dodged a bullet, because I probably would have crumbled under any real criticism." He went on to give an example of positive reinforcement: "I remember doing a collage project of construction paper flowers and I did an unusual leaf in the shape of a heart that showed depth and shadow, and the teacher loved it and showed it to another teacher, which of course made me beam (and seared it into my brain, so that I can recall it today). It would be nice to say that 'creativity is in itself the reward' but in reality, I think the positive reinforcement by others is just as, or more powerful than an internal force."

Avrel recalled his early creations in art and drama: "I presume I was all too happy to show off what I had done and reap praise (some things never change). I never remember being put down over my art. I think about the many times I would recruit my friends and stage elaborate plays on the playground during recess. It was always wildly unrealistic but no one seemed to point that out or to mind playing along." He does, however, remember a painful scene in which he kept asking Carl and me to participate in one of his productions:

"I was, of course, staging a full reproduction of *Jesus Christ Superstar* at the motorcross track [a block from our house], and had been trying to cast you all in it, when I was snapped at: 'If you want to stage a full Broadway production, you're going to have to do it without us.'"

When asked what things might have inhibited him as a child, Erren responded, "I suppose what inhibited me was the cost of things: I remember thinking that a package of markers was the most expensive and valuable thing on the planet. I was afraid to use them because if they were lost or used up, that would be it—for a lifetime. Mainly regarding art materials, I think that if I hadn't perceived them as being as valuable as gold, I might have explored more and used up more. On the other hand, necessity is the mother of invention, and we made a lot of funky things out of paper towel rings and shoe boxes, and that has translated into my being able to make something out of nothing when I have to or want to—like store displays or party decorations or costumes at the drop of a hat."

Two brothers, side by side as equal opportunists, and yet Ansen observed, "I don't recall any impediments to creativity, especially due to our lack of excess money." A parent never knows what might be sinking in deeply with one child while the other is oblivious.

It's not up to parents to be the judge of an artistic endeavor by a child. Praise, encourage, bless? Of course. To let a child's accomplishments be forever the center of attention ("Tots and Tiaras"), to rush them into competition, and to din into them that the ultimate goal is public notice? Absolutely not. Robert Schirrmacher in *Art and Creative Development for Young Children* wisely observed, "It is hoped that young children will not abandon a creative process orientation in favor of making art products that look like something solely to please adults."[2] Well...yes!

We didn't reward our children with money for good grades or dock them for infringements. We didn't want to start that sort of push-pull relationship and besides, we had no money for such. But more than that, it was an understood thing that their best reward was their own sense of pride and accomplishment. We were happy to be bystanders, there to cheer them on or console them when they failed.

Training

A friend of mine was explaining why she had brought her young daughter to church even though she herself had "no feeling for religion." She said her daughter seemed to have a "talent" for spiritual things. What an interesting application of the word!

Who hasn't swooned over the precocious abilities of six-year-old pianists, dancers, preachers, and conductors on YouTube? Our second thoughts after our shock and awe may be a little wistfulness for their futures—Will they be driven? What will they have left to do in their lives, and will those chosen paths satisfy them? Studies show that only a few of these remarkable children go on to be world-class adult artists and entertainers without intensive training.[1] The skill can be instilled by rote and repetition when they are toddlers, but a fleshing out of other character aspects will be needed if this first flash of brilliance is sustained throughout a lifetime.

Some people seem to be born with the natural ability to invent; we may say they are gifted. Others have a bent toward learning and applying skills; they are labeled talented. It surely takes varying portions of both if an individual is to excel in a field of endeavor.

If we think solely about creativity as the act of producing something new, we may not immediately see how skills and performance are a part of that. But there are few adult creators who have not also developed skills, through years of study and practice, that allow them to be even more creative. The research scientist may have brilliant hypotheses but he will need skill and patience to labor day after day in his laboratory if he is to come up with brilliant new conclusions or products. The fundamental skill of typing is practically essential to the professional writer. There may be no obvious product of creativity in the dazzling artistry of some world-class performers, but we onlookers may be sure that creativity has played a major role in the thrilling moment of the skilled display.

There's an implied relationship between the givens of talent and the efforts of skill. The noted author Madeleine L'Engle said, "We can't take any credit for our talents. It's how we use them that counts." [2] I take the liberty here in a book about creativity to tell something of the training that went into the shaping of our sons. I leave it to you to get the connection between a child learning the words for singing in an opera and his adult self doing experimental photography, or running an artful business, or writing a book.

Erren put it this way: "Being in a university and church theater environment gave us lots of exposure to creativity: performance, set building, etc. I forget sometimes how much of a cornerstone that was to our childhood. That was a huge advantage for us: being on the 'inside' of the performing arts."

As noted in their individual stories, Erren and Avrel took art lessons for several years at the McAllen International Museum, and Ansen got an early start in photography from his photography scout troop. These activities required very little effort from us. Pay the fee, get them to their lesson on time, and have a conversation about the results.

The boys' first venture onto the stage came when Erren was 5 and Ansen was 8. Earlier, I mentioned Erren's singing the part of the boy Nicholas in a performance of Benjamin Britten's *Life of Nicholas*. They both chose to try out for this one part and did. Erren was smaller and had a higher crystal-clear voice, so he was picked. We knew there would be a winner and a loser in this audition so we promised the "loser" that he would get a tee shirt of his choice. Ansen chose a light blue sweatshirt with pink velour flowers on the front. Erren said later that he envied Ansen and wished he could have been the loser!

That year Erren also was chosen to play the role of the changeling in Shakespeare's *A Midsummer Night's Dream* produced by the drama department of North Texas State University. He had a cute little costume with a blousy jacket and puffed midcalf Persian pants. And because he was an exotic, this very white little Anglo was made up in rich brown tones. He was to be barefoot but because it was cold backstage, the wardrobe mistress had him keep on his socks and shoes until his first appearance on stage. It was quite a shock to see this little north-African child with shockingly white feet—so white they seemed to glow! Others noticed it, besides his parents, and at his next entrance, his feet were properly brown.

When Erren and Ansen were 9 and 11 respectively, they were cast in the role of the boy Amahl, in *Amahl and the Night Visitors,* a Christmas opera by Gian Carlo Menotti. This was a production of the music department of Pan American University with performances in both English and Spanish. I wrote to my parents, "The boys are in the living room singing the opera at the top of their lungs. They are going through it with the record." Carl taught them their parts, which they seemed to catch on to quickly, even though they had no formal lessons in Spanish. Still, the task took many hours, and there was a cliff-hanger: Almost 12, Ansen had a singing voice on the verge of change. Sure enough, it changed from soprano to alto/tenor literally overnight right after the last performance. He came home from a sleepover at a friend's the next weekend and we had a teenager.

In the mid-70's, Carl undertook a production of *Joseph and the Amazing Technicolor Dreamcoat* with his youth choir of 30 kids at the First Presbyterian Church in McAllen. Ansen was Pharaoh; Erren and Avrel were part of the chorus.

When Erren was 12, he sang the lead role of the boy in Carl's opera *The Atonement.* (And for the 25th anniversary performance of this opera in 2000, Erren played the role of the half-wit who bedeviled the boy.) In a concert staging of Prokofiev's *Peter and the Wolf* in 1974 which Carl conducted with the Valley Symphony, Avrel at 7 played the role of the little old man, with Erren as the eleven-year-old wolf.

One memory of exposing them to culture is from the early 70's when we had moved back to the Valley from graduate school. We took them in the late afternoon one cold day to a reception at the original McAllen Museum, housed in an old stucco building. They were the only children there, three scruffy-looking kids bundled in their winter jackets, and they proceeded to sate their after-school appetites by standing near the refreshment table scarfing down handfuls of crackers and cheese. I had to remind them repeatedly to *move away* from the food!

We both felt that all the boys should know how to play the piano, if for nothing more than to learn to read music. Piano is generally considered basic to proceeding to other musical endeavors. I took lessons throughout my childhood and have enjoyed being able to play for personal pleasure as an adult. Carl was not so lucky with early tutoring, and as a result, he labored unduly in graduate school with his lack of piano proficiency.

So he was especially adamant about the boys' knowing how to play. They all took lessons early on, practicing before school each morning with Carl supervising at their side, his breakfast on a tray. I stayed in the kitchen feeding each boy as he emerged from or before he entered the "practice den." This routine worked well for many months until one morning when Ansen broke under the stern tutelage of his father's "Do it again." He crashed his arms on the piano, stood up, and said he wouldn't play anymore.

That incident was patched up years later when Carl wrote a trombone solo for Ansen, who performed it with his high school band and later at Trinity University in San Antonio when he was a student. After performing "Essence," his dad's composition at Trinity, Ansen wrote Carl a letter which he cherished. It read in part,

I've never felt so overcome with the power of the medium of music, pure and simple, as I feel when I play the opening statements of 'Essence.' And I know that the emotion you feel in that piece is being transmitted through me to the people that are listening at that very moment...This 'Essence' is the essence of you and me and each one of us separately. Perhaps someday, I can show you the same feeling through the medium I am training myself in right now.

Ansen proved his musicality, just not on the piano. He was chosen for two years for the trombone section of the All-State Band, the state's top honor group, and received the Arion Award in high school, the musical equivalent of the high school quarterback award.

Postscript: Ansen's son Luca took piano throughout his youth.

Work

Maybe Ansen's being the first child made him remember well tasks that he and his brothers were required to perform. He names mowing the yard, copying music parts, and practicing piano as shapers for his later constitution for work.

It's interesting that the entire family has an exceptional capacity for work. Could it stem from our Puritan ancestors? The boys acquired jobs on their own in their teens and without prompting. They would just come home and say, "I have a job." When Ansen was a senior in high school, he worked in a steakhouse for a while at night—something I didn't like since he came in late. I also didn't like the fact that he told me the bus boys ate their supper of leftover morsels of steak from customers' plates when they returned to the kitchen with a load of dirty dishes. Erren worked in various departments of an upscale department store on Saturdays and during holidays.

Avrel tried his hand at fast food serving but didn't last long at that. His best jobs were announcing ballgames and taking a DJ shift on the weekends at a local radio station. Both Erren and Avrel worked on occasion at a school supply store, compliments of the benevolent owner-parents of their two best friends.

Reflecting on the sons' eagerness to work, I would assign that trait at least 90% to their need for spending money. As young children, they received a small weekly allowance but as they got older, we didn't have the money to expand that allowance into a sum that would do them any good for their more sophisticated wants.

They also had the example of their parents. Their father and I worked at many different jobs to make money. Years when I was not doing classroom teaching, I typed papers, taught flute and piano lessons, and edited manuscripts. During the boys' growing years, Carl always had a job on Sundays as a church choir director. And he did not mind getting his hands dirty at do-it-yourself carpentry and plumbing around the house. (See "The Pursuit of Happiness" earlier.) He also taught private instrumental lessons and at one time did substitute teaching.

The Puritan work ethic was and still is very strong in our family. All five of us are stubborn about our work: Let us at it! There has never been a sharp division between work and play. Sometimes work seems like play. Luckily, the grown sons all have work that blends their need for play in creativity with the means to make a living. Did they choose what they do for a living as an extension of practicing and playing at their art? It's a plausible possibility.

Discipline

The word "discipline" has wide connotation. It can mean the control of day-to-day activities as well as various forms of punishment for wrongdoing. As I look back on the boys' growing years, it seems we were rather strict parents. If there is a facet of that strictness I regret, it is that we maintained a possibly too-quiet home. "Use your indoor voice" was not yet in the vocabulary of child-rearing; we just told them to pipe down. Noise bothered both Carl and me, Carl because of his quiet personality and me because of frequent migraine headaches. Carl did not like rambunctiousness indoors. I would like to say it was his acute hearing, but he could and often did listen to classical music full blast.

So I went along with his predilection, and not unhappily. Our reasoning was that if we were happy, our children would absorb that happiness from us, if not in the immediate present when they were shushed, at least in the long run. If they bothered us with too much noise, we would be crabby. Hopefully, we didn't take this reasoning beyond the limits of good sense. And they were allowed to scream and fight and holler all they wanted to outside. The large trampoline that we provided them for many years was the hour-after-hour site of many a scream-fest.

Carl's mother gave us some insight into the genetics of Carl's sensitivity. She said that her father, also an orchestra conductor, controlled the behavior of his five children solely with silence and with his eyes. One look from him could straighten out any waywardness. Although not as severe, some of that method obviously spilled over in the DNA of the man's grandson. Come to think of it, that's one major way an orchestra is controlled.

As for me, my mother frequently enjoyed telling anyone around how sensitive I was as a child. She said they had to be careful about correcting me because I would cry at the slightest remonstrance.

There is a name for people like Carl and me, High Sensitives.

Elaine Aron has given us legitimacy in her book *The Highly Sensitive Person*.[1] She allowed those of us for whom the world is *Too Loud, Too Bright, Too Fast, Too Tight*[2] to get over feeling like damaged misfits. Aron feels that in most cases, sensitivity is inherited, but parents will have a great deal of input on the final definition in the child. In other words, there's nature modified by nurture.

When the boys were toddlers, we gave them physical reminders with swats on the behind or legs of things forbidden like running toward the street or disobeying verbal commands of "No!" But as they grew and understood language better, we observed that there was no need to do this anymore.

I know I lost my temper a few times during their youth and swatted them soundly on the backside, usually with the fly swatter, but for the most part, we disciplined by reasoning. We didn't know about time-outs back then, and we didn't send them to their room or ground them. In fact, Avrel asked me one day if we loved them. I was shocked. Why would he even think otherwise? It seems that his friend's parents were grounding his friend over and over for infractions and each time, they told him they were doing it because they loved him!

When the guys got out of line, we talked to them: Did they know what they'd done wrong and why it was wrong? And did they know what they should do next time? Maybe I'm conveniently forgetting, but in retrospect it seems to me they were easily controlled and respectful as children, without a lot of cajoling or promises of threats and rewards. When I observe other parents today in difficult encounters with their young children, I am puzzled about why ours were so easy to raise. No doubt they were a little afraid of us. After all, we had the last word on everything in their lives. Maybe the biggest deterrent at least for most of their childhoods was in knowing that if they did something they knew was wrong, we parents would be sorely disappointed in them.

When I'm sitting here trying to remember specific transgressions, I can only recall that Avrel as a toddler once (and only once) told me to shut up, and Erren once fibbed at bedtime that he'd brushed his teeth, and as a teenager Ansen once took a girl into his room and closed the door.

I know now that as teenagers they did a few dangerous or borderline-illegal things we were unaware of. For example, Erren climbed on open scaffolding with his friend to the 17th floor of a bank under construction downtown. Avrel has admitted in adulthood that he went to Mexico with his friends as a teenager some evenings when he was supposed to be at a sleepover in town. But mostly we knew where they were and with whom and what they were doing. I can only say that for the things they did that were out of line, they did not engage the law, and their vices did not stick into adulthood. For these facts, we were very, very lucky parents.

We were at times criticized and perhaps even feared by the boys' friends because we were the strictest parents of their circle. In one incident, we would not allow the boys to go on a long out-of-town trip with a church group because there was no male chaperone. The boys had to endure some harsh comments from their friends about this.

I am wondering if Carl's and my policies of being very tolerant of their brainstorms, messes, and grandiose plans took the place of their need to defy us, a kind of unspoken bargain between children and parents that leveled the playing field and kept Carl and me from being the enemy. We basically let them do anything that didn't hurt them or others.

In my journal, I find recorded details of a couple of memorable school mornings, one in which (and I am not making this up) Erren took to school a 10-gallon aquarium, aerator, filter, gravel, and a fish bowl. That same morning, and in that same car, Ansen took lasagna for 20. And Avrel climbed aboard resplendent in his bicentennial John Hancock costume.

On the last day of school in 1976, Avrel chose again to wear his John Hancock costume but added three drums, a violin, two colonial hats, a quill pen, and a flag. Erren emerged from the house wearing Elton John glasses, three Mardi Gras necklaces, a fake nose, and a tacky wig adorned with a large green plastic bug. Ansen was the epitome of cool: he chose his Humphrey Bogart shirt that morning. We should have known that these shenanigans were a portent of things to come.

Television

I write to my folks in 1965, "Ansen is calling for me to come watch Lassie swimming through a flood, so I'd better go."

The boys growing up in the sixties and seventies were the first generation to be raised in front of the television set. As teenagers in the fifties, Carl and I had been exposed to those early snow-driven glittery shows like *Your Hit Parade, The Jackie Gleason Show* and *What's My Line?* but we never spent the hours in front of the boob tube that our boys did. Reflecting on their eagerness to watch any and everything we would allow, I would now limit their time in front of the box even more than we did. Still, their viewing was probably in the average or scant category compared to that of their friends.

We didn't have a television until 1963, so Ansen did not watch at all during the first two years of his life. But when Kennedy was assassinated, we bought a TV. Contrary to some households, we didn't have the TV on all day long. In the afternoons after school, the boys could watch an hour or so before supper. Evenings were usually off-limits. Carl was away many nights with rehearsals and I had to dig into the mound of essays an English teacher invariably took home from work. School nights, the boys were busy with homework. If Carl and I watched TV, it was usually *The Tonight Show Starring Johnny Carson.*

Saturday morning....ah, that was saturation time. The boys rose early, got their boxes of Lucky Charms and Pop Tarts—the sugar fest, and sat glued to cartoons until noon. When we finally had them turn off the television, there was an instant rabble-rousing among them—a brothers' dispute, individual noisemaking, or perhaps a minor accident like spilled milk, as they returned to themselves and reality. This immediate example of the power of the tube over our children's reality was unsettling to Carl and me.

Avrel, as the youngest, probably was the greatest influenced of the three boys by the TV. By 1967 when he was born, TV programming had become much more extensive and sophisticated, as well as more intox-icating. Avrel writes charmingly about their TV watching in a chapter in his book *Dude* dubbed "My Third Parent: Ted Turner." He lists his early childhood favorites: *The Bugs Bunny/Road Runner Hour, Little House on the Prairie,* and *Gilligan's Island.* Later, he and his brothers watched, along with us, *Saturday Night Live, Laugh In, The Smothers Brothers,* and *All In the Family.*

Avrel describes our hand-me-down black-and-white TV set with its vertical-hold rolls requiring endless adjustment, the foil-covered UHF antennae loop, and the manual dial that demanded hands-on flipping of the channels. As he recounts these sittings, and as the parent now himself of three sons, he comments, "...one could be forgiven for thinking that my parents were asleep at the switch....There were days when Mom and Dad probably should have kicked us all, and me in particular, outside sooner than they did, but, then as now, we were all living in a rapidly changing media environment and figuring it out as we went along the best we could."

He does give us a break however: "...for all my apparent addiction, I surely watched less than most of my friends. It was common knowledge among them that the Seales watched a lot less TV than most other families, and we didn't even have HBO.... I'll hand it to Mom and Dad for these two saving graces: 1) we never ate a meal in front of the television, and 2) we never had TVs in our bedrooms." [1]

I'll add to those saving graces another: If anybody mentioned or quoted a TV commercial at a meal, he had to get up and forfeit a penny from his allowance into a designated container. This practice resulted in the other two boys saying loudly "Penny! Penny!" at the very mention of the commercial.

Though commercials obviously stuck in their brains, they were highly critical of programming and advertising. I would hear them call out "Fake! Fake!" when they deemed a product was being overrated, or they didn't like the acting of a certain player in a drama. I would ask them why they were watching if they didn't like what they saw and there was never a definitive answer, or a move to turn off the TV. Why didn't I act more decisively at these times? Maybe I was comforted by the fact that they were at least being discerning. Their outbursts were evidence that they were not completely duped by the great flickering eye.

Ansen's early favorite shows were *Lost in Space, Star Trek,*

Captain Kangaroo, and *Sesame Street.* He thought Walter Cronkite was Captain Kangaroo for a while. I can remember one serious altercation with him as he watched *Lost in Space.* We needed to leave for the Wednesday evening church supper so I told him to turn off the TV and go to the car. It was near the end of the episode and he was devastated. He was such an easy child to manage most of the time that I was astounded when he countered me by refusing to turn it off. I don't remember how the stand-off ended, but I'm guessing I relented, let him watch the ending, and we were none the worse for being late.

Mea culpa for letting so much television into our boys' lives. I agree with Ellen Handler Spitz writing in her book *The Brightening Glance: Imagination and Childhood* that electronic media do not often provide programming that stimulates ingenuity, curiosity, and "critical reflection and the patience it inevitably requires."[2] Still, I ask myself if there would not have been a negative effect much worse had they been unable to relate at all to their friends who were watching TV. There were a few pockets of excellence in programming, PBS and science how-to programs. And would they not have been culturally deprived had they not been able to sing the Wagnerian "Kill the wabbit! Kill the waaaabbit!" gained from *The Bugs Bunny Hour?*

Brothers: The Sibling Effect

There was not a strong sense of rivalry or competition among the three boys. Their spats were short-lived and usually solved by a parental ruling on the controversy at hand and/or ordering them into separate corners.

When one was being socially clever and entertaining, usually regaling the adults in the room, and another tried to get in on the admiration and suddenly piped up with an addition, they would accuse the interloper with "Improvement!" This came to be a rather useful tool to squelch the rival entertainer.

They had their share of unique coinings. "Rowdy-dow and loudy-dow" meant that the situation was all tied up, solved. A drawn-out "Daaah-oooooh!" was the brag-taunt of a child who had gotten the upper hand.

When I asked them about the influence having brothers might have made on their art, they came up with quite different answers. Ansen observed, "Being the oldest, I never really felt the need to 'keep up' as I think the others do. This may just be my overactive ego at work. I do admire Erren's and Avrel's abilities and energy."

Erren wondered how a Seale child without artistic leanings would have felt in our family. He reflected on his feeling of a running contest in his head between boys "to see who could shine the brightest." Once a category (like writing or photography) was claimed, another brother couldn't "star" in that category. Maybe, he says, his "twisted logic" made him feel he should stay off Ansen's territory so Ansen would stay off of his. "Why I thought that photography or writing or rock polishing or making movies was off limits is beyond me now—not that I have excelled at those things, but it seems funny that I had put up those road blocks when no one asked me to."

Avrel, the youngest, comments, "I'm sure the effect of siblings is profound at innumerable levels, but I also think, in my case, it was mostly unconscious. One image that comes to mind is that of Erren helping me write and illustrate our story books when I was too young to really have done it on my own. That was a very direct example of nurturing creativity though I'm guessing it was not conscious on his part either."

Avrel goes on to say, "I was the third child to come along and so there's an element of this behavior just being the norm. I didn't have to blaze any trails; I just had to fall in line to be considered creative. I don't remember any tones of peer pressure or competition."

An interesting mélange of opinions. Ansen as oldest felt above the fray. Erren as middle child made distinctions on territories. Avrel as youngest just fell in line.

Collaborations

In an article in *The New York Times Book Review* years ago titled "Can This Collaboration Be Saved?" the authors observe that "writing in tandem is a little like two people walking a tightrope while holding hands."[1]

Working together on projects has always been a major part of the Seale family cohesion. Although the emphasis of this book is on the sons, I want to begin by airing some of Carl's and my collaborations as a means of demonstrating—for whatever it might be worth—the fact that working together was a norm for us and something the sons saw modeled in our household.

Probably there's no better place to start than to say that for a vocal solo for our wedding in 1958, I wrote the lyrics which Carl set to music. Carl also wrote the incidental music for piano which preceded the service.

Through the years, we managed to work together on a number of projects involving his music and my words. These include his settings for a number of my poems, a youth musical *The Bible Beasts' Parade*, a dozen hymns, and a song cycle for children's choir.

In the 1980's, we worked several years to produce a kit for Texas classrooms that contained six plays of lesser known heroes and heroines of Texas history. These included a set of songs, one for each play, which Carl composed, notated, and arranged to have recorded by an elementary school choir for an accompanying tape. Out of that material came a set of six easy-to-read books with cartoon illustrations drawn by Carl, these dubbed *The Texas History Biography Series*. We sold these two collaborations to Texas schools for about ten years, actually getting our seed money back and making a small profit.

Working together on artistic projects has definite advantages: sharing the work, pain, money, glory, blame, and liability. When one is down, the other offers encouragement; each gains impetus by the stimulation and vision of the other.

Still, harnessed together, the two find themselves subject to the whims, fortunes, and moods of the other. Often, one must wait out the time limitations of the other. And of course, the illusive-at-best personal voice of the singular artist is sacrificed.

Working on an art project with a family member requires lots of respect. Family members know each other better than they do outsiders but may find themselves caring too much for the other's feelings to move ahead boldly with an assignment.

When a musician and a lyricist work together, the order is always words first, then music. This means the musician has the final say. In our case, I sometimes was asked to agree to a change in the words to fit the metrics of the tune. After we agreed on the general nature of our collaboration, most of our discussions centered around this issue. Sometimes I agreed with his suggestions; other times, it was back to the drawing board.

Already mentioned earlier is Avrel and Erren's collaboration on storybooks, with Avrel telling the story to Erren, who wrote it down and illustrated it. Later, when Avrel formed his rock band in high school, Erren designed the logo for them: THE PLAN.

After college, when the guys' work began in earnest, their needs caused them to call on each other for their various aspects of expertise. Erren asked Ansen to photograph the cover of a cookbook which he designed, *Mesquite Country*, the Museum of South Texas History cookbook published in 1996 and winner of the national Tabasco Community Cookbook Award, as well as to furnish the photo images for brochures and advertising material of his accounts. Through the years, Erren has proved to be a fine booking agent, often hooking up Avrel or Ansen with a writing or photographic project he has knowledge of.

Carl and Ansen have worked together on several major productions of music and photography. "Winged Adventure," showcasing Texas birds, featured Carl's orchestral music played while Ansen's photos were projected on a giant screen above the orchestra. "Jewels of a Land Alive" was Carl's original orchestral suite accompanying Ansen's high-tech display of still and moving images of South Texas wildlife. Carl's final production before retirement was a tour of Rio Grande Valley history in drama, song, and dance named "Our Land: Timeless Valley" which featured Ansen's multi-media theatrical back-drops. Through the years of these productions, Carl asked Erren for publicity materials and Erren complied with beautiful posters and brochures.

In 2004, Avrel asked Carl to write the music for his indie movie production, *The Secret of Suranesh* as well as to play the role of an ancient wise man. (See the appendix for Avrel's account.)

As for my arty interactions with the boys, they have all three been enthusiastic and delightful cohorts. Erren has provided the publisher with cover art and design for six of my books and text illustrations for two of them. The brevity of that simple sentence belies the many hours that such an undertaking consumes.

In 2005, Ansen and I brought to print *Valley Ark*, a collaborative book of fifty poems with coordinating photo images featuring the flora and fauna of the Rio Grande Valley. This has been a very popular book. At readings someone in the audience usually asks which came first, the poem or the photo. I tell them that sometimes I wrote the poem while looking at Ansen's picture and sometimes he had to go tramping through the woodlands to find the animal or plant of my poem. I believe I had the easier job.

Avrel and I enjoy performing together on guitar and flute. We've also presented programs on the mother/son relationship. We share membership in a mutual help society of two, each encouraging the other in our writing. I admire his ability to generate copy and have laughed so hard I cried at some of the things he's written, particularly about growing up in our wacky household and now about raising his three sons.

To conclude, I feel our family has been very lucky to have re-mained in close physical proximity, that is, within traveling distance (McAllen, San Antonio, Austin), to be able to plan and execute our joint projects, even though, more and more, our collaborations are done electronically.

I would not leave the reader thinking that all was peachy in our family's collaborations. There were at times exasperation, short tempers, storming, and stalemates. There were micro-managing, jealousy, and mutterings. There were rethinking and even abandon-ments. But as Bernays and Kaplin concluded in their article in *The New York Times Book Review*, "...as we went about transforming our ideas and raw materials into a book, we saw that two heads, undeniably different and often stubborn, could sometimes be better than one."

In latter years, as our sons have entered busy mid-careers, they have had less time to interact with Carl and me, the ones without regular jobs and thus with more time to dream and create. At times they are just too busy for what we might want to do with them. In most cases, they have kindly acquiesced, humoring us and without major blow-ups. We still practice, each to each, and whatever the combination, an old-fashioned behavior: we *abide* each other.

Faith

When our three boys were small, they maintained more than a speaking acquaintance with God. Nothing was too sacred, inappropriate, or trivial to approach God about. No observation on God's nature was sacrilegious; they cultivated a strictly informal friendship with the Deity.

There was one period when a boy chastened God in his nightly prayers for not filling in human navels so stomachs could be smooth. Also during this time, this child continually thanked God for the fact that his little brother cried when he was scared.

At mealtime, God was thanked retroactively, presently, and prospectively for all the beans and peas in the world, regardless of whether they were on the menu.

Training in Bible stories started early. When Ansen was two years, three months, he came in with a blanket over his head, wanting a kiss and a hug because he was leaving. I inquired where he was going. The answer: "To Bethlehem." When I asked the purpose of the mission, he replied, "I'm gonna' get some peanut butter." Who said religion wasn't practical!

Once at Christmas, when we were attempting to stress the spiritual rather than the material of the season, a tot listened quietly to our reasoning, then observed, "God may be the greatest but Santa is the funnest." Ansen, 10, during his fishing period, and too old for a Santa wish list but not too sophisticated for hope, went around singing the tune of "Silent Night" substituting "Ro-od 'n reel, ro-od 'n reel."

Erren made quite an issue of Bible stories. He had special names for those characters who impressed him. Doh-Doh Goliath was his favorite villain and Big Dave—Doh-Doh's slayer—his hero. Once he came home wonderingly from Sunday School with the news that Jonathan had given Big Dave an arrow and a panty girdle [The Biblical girdle was a power belt] as a friendship present.

Avrel passed through a long and imaginative Old Testament period. One day, at four years old, our Noah was standing atop a pile of laundry, stretching forth his yardstick to call all the animals into the ark. Carl called His Eminence to lunch. The child turned royally to him, and in a pious voice remonstrated, "You may not speak to me in English. Speak to me only in 'Holy.'"

As they grew older, they didn't seem quite as frank with God as they formerly were. But religious training and church were never optional with them while they were at home with us. Even if they felt the natural conflicts of simple childlike faith colliding with teenage doubt, they were required to go regularly to church. And most of the time, they willingly complied, even if only to see their friends, also being raised in the faith.

Lest we sound too pious about church attendance, let it be noted that their father was, in their growing years, the choir director of several Protestant churches, a second job that kept us in town, particularly on weekends. Also, perhaps because my father was a minister, I felt confident with accepting various teaching roles in the church, as well as being active in the music. We were *there*, and they had to be too.

As teens, Sunday nights offered a weekly chance to get together with their friends in the church and play volleyball, eat supper, and participate in discussions relevant to their daily living, moral fiber, and social issues like peace and justice. Additionally, there were lock-ins, midwinter retreats, summer camps, and cross-country trips that were well-sponsored and in which they gladly participated.

The church youth groups distinguished themselves by always having a benevolent cause. They stayed busy holding lawn sales, washing cars, and hosting adult suppers, sometimes to raise money for their own traveling to national youth assemblies but often to help the less fortunate. They occasionally went into Mexico, along with adults, to lend their muscle to building homes and schools, or visited poor areas here in the Valley with food and gifts for families.

As for exercising their creativity in these groups, their wise tireless leaders gave them free rein, or nearly so, to do their own thing. They made posters, decorated for banquets, played their instruments for worship and Easter sunrise services, and acted in dramas (usually having a great time outfitting themselves from a big closet at church kept expressly for that purpose). One notable yearly observance was transforming the fellowship hall, second floor area, and organ loft into a Halloween atmosphere for the amusement of the congregation at their annual fall celebration.

Every three months, they designed their own worship service. For these, they wrote their own sermon and prayers, arranged their music, and executed the whole hour.

I cannot stress enough how important these times were to our boys' growing up. Of course, Carl and I were not so naïve as to think that our children were paragons of virtue. But we did know where they were during many of their waking hours, and we were very fortunate in being able to trust the youth leaders of our church.

During the 70's and 80's, the time of their teens, there were perhaps fewer opportunities to drop into the drug, alcohol, and gang world than there are today. By their own admission, they sometimes landed in environments where these were temptingly presented.

Still, by that time they knew from the guidance of their youth leaders, the teachings of the church, and their parents' expectations that such things weakened character and eroded a happy future. Participation in them would draw sanctions from the adults around them that they respected and wanted to please.

If all this sounds a little lofty and smug, I emphasize that they were safely programmed for many, many waking hours by activities under the umbrella of church; their very winsome youth leaders, as well as Carl and I, held up to them daily, even pestered and cajoled them, with the ideals of the Christian faith; and we were just plain lucky that they squeaked through the teen years with their characters intact.

As adults, they have chosen individual ways to express their faith. I assume not any of them are regretful of their growing years spent in the church.

Although today our sons would probably decline a test on Biblical knowledge, in those arbitrary years of church attendance, we believed our children were acquiring a basis for appreciating their spiritual heritage. Children who are "churched" may acquire a layer of Judeo-Christian history and culture valuable to them later in life. Ours learned stories of the Bible, accounts agreeably not taught in public school, but which make living the richer. They understand allusions in literature and art that they would not otherwise know—the plight of Job, the road to Damascus, Daniel in the lion's den, the journey of the Magi, Jonah and the whale, and the feeding of the 5,000.

To know the famous Bible stories of storms, escapes, wild

animals, healings, trustings, rulers, slaves, right and wrong behavior—these form a matrix for understanding allusions in literature and culture, great visual art, and glorious music.

Some might ask what all this had to do with creativity. I think it grounded them socially so that they associated with like-minded young people. And I believe their early indoctrination in faith, with its tenet of relying on the Divine, has given them a humble perspective on their gifts.

Yes, many other influences and happenings have been mentioned in this book, but in the end, an area of Causation, of Mystery, something that is not of their or our parental efforts, is part of the Neither of the title.

Part Five: Considerations

Introduction

The nature vs. nurture conversation is far from over or one-sidedly conclusive. Of course it takes both, and that will likely not change as a fact. Still, fascinating results of current research keep us guessing at the outcome. Is the DNA inexorably set? How much nurture and of what type? Does neither play an important role in the personality of a child "fated," as it were, to be an artist?

By now you may have come to your own conclusions about raising creative children. Or given this uneven and whimsical manifesto, you could be more confused than ever. I offer a few observations for further contemplation, even clarification. Some of my observations are 20/20 hindsight; some are testimonials as to how our kids turned out. I leave it to you—parents, teachers, and friends—as to what to believe and what to counter, all according to your own unique children.

Genes

If I had to make a quick call on the inherited genes of our children, I'd say the boys got from Carl his emotional steeliness, work ethic, visual artistry and music. From me they got a passion for ideas, love of words, a sense of humor, and music.

Michael Rutter, a developmental psychopathologist, believes that genes are "probabilistic rather than deterministic."[1] For the question "How much has your present interest and participation in your art been influenced by heredity?" our sons had very different answers. Ansen felt that heredity had played only a very small part, five percent. Erren credited his genes with 49 percent of his artistry, and Avrel split the difference, with a value of 30 percent for his DNA.

When I look at these percentages, I am made aware that identical parentage, similar upbringing, and correspondence of life values may imprint quite differently on three siblings.

Very interesting recent gene research has to do with epigenetics. This is the study of how genes can be switched on and off dependent on environment and experiences. "Epi-" as a prefix means "on top of," with the implication being that of effects in addition to or coming out of DNA strands. Here is where the experience of parents comes in. It seems that epigenetic markers block developing fetal cells from following any genetic instructions that don't match their intended roles. This biochemical process occurs not just during gestation and early fetal development but throughout one's life. It is shocking to know that "parental behaviors that occur long before pregnancy may influence an offspring's well-being."[2] The most obvious changes, and the ones that can be more readily observed, are those occurring near or during pregnancy. A pregnant woman's faulty diet may cause epigenetic changes linked to increased brain and spinal cord defects in children. Pregnant women traumatized by 9/11 had a greater incidence of giving birth to infants with high levels of fear and stress when faced with loud noises and unfamiliar people.[3]

I ask myself how my children's genes might have been affected by events prior to their birth. Could it be that Ansen's DNA was influenced by my emersion in academics? How about Erren? Shortly before I became pregnant with him, I took a powerful antibiotic for an infection. With Avrel, before his birth, it was surely a ride on the Sombrero at Six Flags amusement park when I became so ill on the dips and rises that my six year old--for crying out loud--had to console me, pat my arm, and assure me that we'd be back on the ground soon. I leave my sons to figure out how these dips and rises in the outer bands of my DNA strands might have affected their dispositions, predilections, fears and strengths. And that's just their mother. I cannot begin to conjure the variables from their father's contribution.

Right- or Left-Brain Dominance

Not long ago a neurologist meeting Carl and me for the first time and knowing something of our professions said, "Ah, two right-brained people!" He was kind enough (and maybe covering his remark) to go on to comment that the world needed more of our type.

For about fifty years, the idea of brain lateralization has been a convenient way for psychologists and others to describe thinking processes and learning patterns. The theory goes that people whose left half of the brain is dominant are logical, rational, analytical, and objective while people with right brain dominance are creative, emotional, intuitive, and subjective.

Recent iterations of this concept have brought us nearer the truth: we need both sides if we are to function as fully realized adults even though our behavior, and even our handedness and eye-ness, seem to indicate that one side or the other of the brain is our main guide.

If the theory is correct, with creativity as important to all in our family as it is, we may assume that we five are essentially right-brained. Still, there are certain exceptions and anomalies in this label for us. For example, many right-brained people are left-handed, the assumption being that the right side of the brain controls the left side of the body. I am the only left-handed person of us five. I am also the only one of us with a dominant left eye. Whether I am more right-brained than the others is not at all certain, although one memorable comment by Erren when he was 10 put the kibosh on any doubts: "Let's face it, Mom, you're no Einstein." My left-side indications could simply mean that I was damaged at birth, since in truth I did have a very precarious entry into this world. Or it could mean that the right and left lobes of my brain are switched in their placement. Or neither.

Ansen is quite good in math and uses it daily in photographic calculations. At one time math was thought to be a decidedly left-brain function and recently proven to be strongest when both halves of the brain work together. Avrel, Erren, and I are the "word nerds," with language proficiencies, a seeming left-brain function.

I would make a caveat to our right-brain majority, however, in that we all appear to have enough concourse between the two sides that our left brain is able to help us solve problems, keep us from stepping into traffic, and allow us to balance our bank statements.

One learning weakness is probably worth mentioning, only because of its peculiar manifestation in Carl. With dyslexia rampant on his family's side, Carl especially had trouble with reading as a child, though he apparently kept it a secret and dyslexia was not commonly recognized at the time. He reported that the letters jumped around and it was difficult when reading a page to revert to the next line of type. He wryly commented that he didn't start to make "A's" in school until he worked on his graduate degrees, by that time figuring out what he needed to do in order to be able to get through the reading. We may marvel how a person with dyslexia was able to become an orchestral conductor, since reading a musical score of eighteen instrumental parts simultaneously is standard for the calling.

Sensitivity

When I was a child, I cried easily, feared the dark, and stayed troubled for months by unsettling scenes or stories. I was admonished not to be "so sensitive." The stigma of sensitivity was to remain with me into adulthood, when gradually I began to see that this trait had a positive side. I noticed more things; my senses were sharper; my observations could be of value. I became a writer.

The psychotherapist Elaine Aron has combined solid research with clinical insights to produce *The Highly Sensitive Person*, a life-saving volume with the subtitle "How to Thrive When the World Overwhelms You." Among many unique traits of Highly Sensitive People, "intuition is right often enough that HSPs tend to be visionaries, highly intuitive artists, or inventors, as well as more conscientious, cautious, and wise people."[1] There is burden and blessing in this, but we and our sons definitely wear the label.

Aron writes of levels of arousal, the gauge of the nervous system's tolerance to stimuli. Too much and the person is agitated, troubled, confused. Too little brings on lethargy and ineffectiveness. The right amount of arousal is the best of all states of being, and this right amount is quite different for different people.

Within a species, the percentage that is very sensitive to stimulation is usually around 15-20 percent. I believe those in the arts are almost altogether a part of this percentage. Here is where "being inspired" comes from—a happy, tailor-made state of arousal. It is said that in monkey colonies, twenty percent are sent to the top of the canopy in the rain forest to be lookouts—aroused to note rival colonies, danger of all sorts, and the location of food. If the artist's role includes helping to preserve culture, we can see that the metaphor—even the fact of our species kinship—of the treetop monkeys applies to artists. I always want to be one of those treetop monkeys.

A passage from my journal of some years back:

Tending soul: that is the real job. I think that is what all our family was put on this earth for. The boys certainly all do that:

Ansen—his photography is a statement—this is how things are; behold, think, live fuller, know the bone-and-soul 3-D of images;

Erren—his store is not about things so much as it is about customers' yearnings for connections—this candle is to call up Spirit; that milagro creates remembrance; this picture is given as a gift and a connection to others;

Avrel—ideas; how to help people think; what their realities are; who he is and who we are.

Personalities

When Ansen and Erren engage in family analysis, they often jokingly label themselves as Ansen the introvert, Erren the extrovert, and Avrel, the ambivert, "the one Mom and Dad finally got it right on." Actually, I think they are all introverts by varying degrees but all three possessed with what Susan Cain, in her book titled simply *Quiet,* calls high self-monitoring. Introverts with high self-monitoring skills have true solitary natures but can sense appropriate behavior when they need to interact with others. Their preference is to stay on the edge of the crowd but they know when they must step forward into the limelight and to what degree the world needs them, and they are not above enjoying this social interaction. Their high self-monitoring is not the same as pretending or acting. Rather, it is regulating their inner natures to a satisfactory degree for their own well being and the comfort of those around them. [1]

It is interesting to note that Ansen's and Erren's chosen life work has consisted of self-employment—Ansen's photography studio and Erren's advertising design business and then his cultural arts store. And although Avrel has usually been salaried, both of his major adult jobs, first in magazine editing and now in speechwriting, demand solitary thinking and writing time, as does his avocation of producing books. Avrel thinks of himself as "an occasional extrovert." He can call up his extrovert nature when it's needed but it is not the default setting. Additionally, all three sons select very carefully their group activities, with none being a first-class joiner of clubs and associations.

In family conversation someone once noted that at one time we all lived in houses built on a corner (escape routes? grander lots?). That's still true, except for Ansen, who has since moved into an old neighborhood in San Antonio on a triple lot with much seclusion and no houses across the street. Could there be an introvert implication in these nesting choices?

Cain gives many engaging histories of well-known people—professors, business tycoons, actors—who are at heart introverts but have made major impacts on their worlds and society in general. It is her contention that introverts have been given short shrift in the spotlight but more often than not control the movement of culture.

Carl Jung averred, "There is no such thing as a pure extrovert or a pure introvert. Such a man would be in the lunatic asylum."[2] High self-monitoring is the ability to take in one's surroundings and adjust one's behavior to the appropriate degree of social engagement. We can readily see how an introvert with little or no self-monitoring might be described as shy and withdrawn, while one with high self-monitoring could be outwardly amiable, pleasant, and engaging, while still enjoying going home from the party.

Humors and Muses

Another useful way of defining personality is by using the ancient Greek terms for the four temperaments, or humors, as they were called: sanguine, choleric, melancholic, and phlegmatic, especially as they have evolved through the ages into modern-era iterations. These labels are very helpful for analyzing new acquaintances and old friends. Their properties keep one from the good-bad, lovable-hateful designations that so often crop up in our opinions about others. They keep us from making snap judgments about new acquaintances and help us to tolerate some behaviors in the longtime ones.

In terms of the Greek and later medieval humors, Ansen is a phlegmatic—relaxed, quiet, content with himself, non-judgmental. Of our sons, the one who comes closest to being a true introvert, in their mother's opinion, is Ansen. Ansen is happiest working by himself developing something he has dreamed up, usually in the world of photography. His early photo images were of things rather than people. I have teased him about having a chair fetish, with a number of images with the subject of chair in his portfolio—chairs fitted into gondolas, solitary forgotten ones on plazas, grouped chairs visiting together in retirement home gardens.

Still, his commercial art livelihood requires him to interact with the social, cultural and business world. He works on assignment in—as he puts it— "pillows, perfume, pet food and anything else somebody wants to sell." In these situations, he is comfortably amiable. He is also cool when he is making a presentation, with very little evidence that here before a crowd explaining the relationship of motion to time in digital photography stands a man who'd prefer to be in his studio scratching the belly of the studio cat and thinking about his next invention. Ansen inherited the *sangfroid*, the coolness of mind and composure of his father.

Some who know Erren may think I've surely gotten it wrong that I peg him too as an introvert. Sanguines are talkative, not shy, and often witty. They are warm-hearted, impulsive and charismatic. Erren is all of these. But he's still a high self-monitoring introvert. Even though Erren is highly sociable and pleasure-seeking, defining in behavior the sanguine temperament of the four ancient humors, he has a side that is deeply cogitative and solitary. Sometimes he reports on his Facebook page that he has spent a perfect afternoon alone working in his garden and then floating in his pool staring up at the sky. At these times he is calling for his space. If one can be an introvert and also sanguine, Erren is a good example.

Wherever Erren goes, he can make a party. I suspect that he would rather improvise a good time than methodically plan one, but he can do either, and does so frequently until he says, "Enough!" and opts to drive across New Mexico alone, or stroll through quaint secondhand stores in burgs up and down I-35.

Of the humors designations, Avrel strikes me as a melancholic. These folks are ponderers, very considerate of others, and self-reliant and independent. Melancholics can be creative in the arts—certainly a trait of Avrel's as he writes books and performs quite successfully on the guitar.

And, yes, the other two sons probably have Avrel figured out as a blend of themselves. Avrel is also an introvert, again a high self-monitoring one who is required by his career to spend many hours alone with words at his computer but also to interact with adminis-trators and to be a public speaker at the university and at Bahá'í gatherings. He actually enjoys speaking and often gives original presentations emanating from the book he is writing at the time or from his spiritual faith. Avrel, of the three, is the one most fully involved in social media. He posts often on Facebook and blogs with full essays on various topics. I have written earlier of his shyness as a child; this has not seemed to carry over as an adult.

So... I will stick to my motherly guns that they are all three introverts who nevertheless monitor themselves closely because they need and want social interaction. Their differences are more nearly epitomized by the ancient system of humors, with its iterations by interpreters through the ages suggesting personality types. A "phleg," a "sang," and a "mel"—certainly not all-encompassing of the person-alities, but at least useful.

Along with the temperaments, the smart Greeks also articulated another human label, that of those visited by the Muses, who brought the creative spark to humans. In a blog titled "Daily OM," one writer observes that "we may have one muse that remains with us throughout our lives, multiple muses that inspire us concurrently, several muses that come and go as necessary, or a single muse that touches us briefly at specific moments."[1]

Not to oversimplify the adult states of our sons, it seems to me that Ansen's muses are faithful ones accompanying him at all times, while Erren's muses come and go as he bids them, and Avrel's inspire him concurrently.

Part Six: Cultivating Creativity

Introduction

What inner voice urges us on to create new pictures, sculpture, stories, poems, symphonies? Is there anything truly new under the sun? Is art simply rearrangement of past creations?

Artistic creativity is hard to explain and hard to measure. That is why I have taken in this book mostly an anecdotal approach in writing about family creativity.

If easy answers were available about raising creative children, we would go straight to those rather than chronicling the sometimes strange but more often ordinary course of a family which happened to be devoted to the arts.

There is much Carl and I will never know about why all our sons turned to the arts for the main activity of their lives. The following pronouncements are an attempt to articulate what does seem knowable to me. If these observations are interesting or helpful to anyone else—parent, teacher, child influencer—I am glad.

Creativity Can Flourish in Family Life

Ellen Spitz writes in *The Brightening Glance* that children "do not separate these [dance, theater, music, literature, and visual arts] out subjectively from other aspects of their lives—from their ordinary excursions, their living and play spaces, their holidays...perceiving and imagining go hand in hand in early childhood...To a child, these realms feel seamless."[1] As Avrel put it, "We were free to pursue whatever creative path we were called to. We never thought about it in those terms, of course."

With this realization, it's possible to see how Mom's and Dad's creative activities in the home would seep into the deep consciousness of a growing child. Of our home atmosphere, Avrel commented, "I think positive example, or the 'norming' of creativity was probably a big factor in my case."

When Carl wrote *The Atonement*, his opera which starred a boy child of about 10 years of age, he had in mind Ansen and Erren, ages 11 and 9 respectively. While reading various sources and thinking about the plot, he was delighted when he came across Chaucer's "Prioress's Tale" because it featured a child (even though he had to do a major rewrite of the plot because it contained anti-Semitism).

I was not much on baking cookies or planning the Halloween festival for the boys' classes but I sometimes wrote poems for them. I can remember writing a poem that included one couplet on each of the children in Erren's third-grade class. He helped me with the details on each child. Another time I wrote a Thanksgiving poem featuring Native Americans which Erren illustrated, took to school, and had all the class chanting.

Not only do children incur deep subconscious feelings about the arts when their surrounding adults manifest them and participate in them, but there's a pay-off for adults. Parents and teachers get to be children again, fleshing out some of their unfulfilled childhood in socially acceptable ways when they play artistically with their children.

141

What adult has not smiled in guilty pleasure at playing a duet or coloring delicately (or viciously) a picture with a child? The arts provide a level ground for all ages.

If you enjoy landscaping, talk about it with your child. If you like making up recipes for cookies, clown around in the kitchen with a kid. Don't feel that you can share only some high art or that you must save your artistic hobbies until your children are grown. Here is an area where you don't have to pontificate, as so much of being a parent consists of.

And if you, in your own art, have come up against an obstacle, share what you can of that. Children need to see vulnerability and appropriate chance-taking in their parents. Ansen observed to me, "As a kid, I remember your rejection letters from publishers, so I knew what I was in for when it came my turn to compete." At times I must have been pretty open with my wailing. Kids are listening up.

Carl Jung, the great psychoanalyst, reasoned that a major source of creativity derives from the collective thoughts of our ancestors. His premise was more than simply history teaching lessons or a grand-mother showing a grandchild a skill. His was a vision that we have a creative collective DNA that we all inherit. It is up to us as parents and teachers to let it shine forth around our children.

Hardship, Adversity, and Risk-taking
Can Be Plus Factors

Earlier in the book I have spoken about our limited financial means when the boys were young. We were not dirt poor but we certainly had to be very careful with money in all aspects of our lives. I like to think of our financial means as one where we went to Luby's cafeteria once a month but the boys were not allowed to get sodas, milk, or dessert. These were the days when we took the beginning-of-school supply lists and first ranged across the house rounding up used pencils, ballpoint pens, and half-used spiral notebooks before repairing to the store to flesh out the rest. Ours was a genteel poverty.

Except for Erren's feeling that colored markers were not to be used because they were too expensive to ever be replaced (!), the sons did not seem to notice our limited means, and in some cases, their creativity actually increased because they had to entertain themselves (these days called "free, non-directed play") and with very few manufactured toys.

Of adversity, I would cite my being sidelined in bed for two years with tuberculosis when I was ready to start school as being a definite plus putting me on the road to contemplation and the love of learning. When Carl was in college, he survived on one meal a day. Erren's three-year stint in his scoliosis brace put him to the test and gave him a tensile strength during the fragile teenage years.

We'll never be able to say with surety how our going to graduate school affected our three children. Certainly we did graduate school in the wrong order—three children and *then* back for more study. Perversity created adversity. We were one of those families where the menu the last week of the month contained lots of beans as well as mayonnaise (*no mas*) sandwiches. Once when Carl was highly frustrated with one of his courses, Erren, then five, picked up on it, struck a defiant pose and declared, "I'll tell you one thing: I'm *never* going to get my doctor's degree."

We took a risk moving away from the Valley for four years and another risk returning to it. But our geographic isolation upon our return—away from big-city distractions and culture—caused us to be more active in the arts than we might have been otherwise. We had to make our own art, not depend on decades of artistic endeavor ahead of us.

In 1977, I was part of a movement to form a literary magazine in the Valley with the title of *riverSedge*. Early on, I wrote an editorial there entitled, "Art in the Boonies," in which I defended our art-making in the hinterland. "We have no overlay of literati or high society to cater to," ..."we are never surfeited with art." Still, there was plenty to do. "Dance program, art exhibit, chamber concert, play, recital, poetry reading—we can be there in ten minutes; we can usually take our children; the cost is little or nothing."[1]

Allowing some limited risk-taking for children may be conducive to creating strengths in them that would otherwise not develop. In an article in *Ode* magazine titled "We don't need no supervision," the author Tim Gill points out that for our children there's a "value in tasting freedom." He suggests that "the over-regulation of children's lives has a big downside" and that "we can reject the culture of overprotection and come up with practical steps to give our children more responsibility."[2] Of course, we love our children and want to protect them from serious threats, but we need to help children build their coping mechanisms.

Experimenting in the arts, for better or for worse, is one fail-safe way to allow our children a bit of a tussle with the universe, one that they'll someday meet head-on in other areas of their lives.

High IQ and Good Grades Are Not Synonymous with Creativity

Einstein averred, "Imagination is more important than knowledge."[1] In *How Children Succeed*, Paul Tough makes a case for grit, curiosity, and the power of character as determinants for helping children grow into strong adults. He observes,

"Pure IQ is stubbornly resistant to improvement after about age eight. But executive functions [reasoning] and the ability to handle stress and manage strong emotions can be improved, sometimes dramatically, well into adolescence and even adulthood."[2]

All our boys have healthy IQs but they did not choose to shine academically, making mostly good grades when it was convenient. In high school, Ansen made a C+ in math...the self-same year he was president of the McAllen High School Math Club! Some people say boys are less obsessed with making good grades than girls and I tend to agree. Although all three boys made good grades, they didn't choose academics as a way of shining. Achievement seems to have been reserved for their arts.

Competition in the Arts Can Be Helpful, Destructive, or Meaningless

Much depends on the nature of the child. If an art instructor or parent always praises one child but never the one beside him, that second will face an uphill battle to move forward using his natural ability. He will probably need an obsession or an abundant amount of ego to see him through the destructiveness of this silent competition.

Our sons did not give competition very high marks. Ansen says he wrote off competitiveness early on because he was never very good at sports. "In music it was all about playing the right notes in the right order, so, not much creativity there either." Thinking further about "the early beatings I took in sports," he noted that these probably contributed positively to a trait that has held him in good stead as he has had to compete in the art world. "I can shake off disappointment when I don't get into some show or receive a grant."

Years ago, when Erren had his own design studio, he enjoyed winning Addys, the best in categories of advertising in this region's advertising association. As time went on, winning became routine, with less zing, up until he quit the commercial art business. He is still fiercely competitive in the community drama club he belongs to and enjoys in turn producing, directing, and acting in plays that may win him a trophy at the annual "Academy Awards" the club holds each spring. On the plus side, Erren comments that "competitive spirit gets the adrenaline going, to maximum benefit."

Avrel was in childhood highly competitive, and he claims now that in "meaningless games I still am." But he sees no connection between competitiveness and creativity and notes that there might even be a negative correlation. He enjoys watching competitive sports but tends to find competition in the arts "somewhat silly."

De-emphasize competition? Yes, if it's final and destructive. No, if it's inspiring one to strive harder or acting as a filtering process to eliminate choices.

Creativity Is a Process that Follows
a Predictable Pattern

I was tending the seven-year-old daughter of a friend. The child and I walked out into the backyard and she picked up a small stick and a leaf and began to weave the stick into the leaf. "I'm being creative," she announced. She recognized and could name the activity. I felt two ways about that. She recognized the activity but was that a good thing, seeing it as a specific category of brainwork at so early an age? Her mother was an artist, a careful mother and highly articulate. No doubt the child had been exposed to the mechanics of creativity early on.

I'm fairly sure we did not talk systematically to our children about the nature of creativity. Maybe we thought it was so illusive that it was better not to over-explain it: the muses might retreat. After their childhoods, I gave workshops on creativity and at that time began to see the advantages of openly discussing the steps in the creative process, at least with older children.

For younger children, we should be careful not to over-talk the process, so much so that the child begins using left-brain critiquing in the middle of a rush of right-brain creativity. We want them to think fleetingly about what is happening in the six steps of creation, and to use whatever reasoning will help them to be patient within any one step of the process and move toward accomplishment.

These steps can be applied to both artistic creation and ordinary daily problem-solving:

1) The aha! moment. The idea, problem, or challenge is recognized. Let's say the child decides to paint a picture of the family dog.

2) A first period of work. The child sketches the dog in a certain posture.

This is usually fast and easy, and even with a touch of euphoria. Insights follow other insights; new questions present themselves. The brain is having fun!

3) A second period of work. Here, will power has to kick in.

There's deeper inquiry, with harder questions. The child feels the need to position the dog in an environment, so will it be the couch inside or the doghouse outside? Maybe she gets interested in drawing a tree nearby with sky in the background. Maybe she begins to imagine what's involved in completing the work.

4) The problem phase. An optional but highly probable phase occurs: the creator is puzzled, stumped, stalled. Perhaps our dog artist mistakenly becomes mesmerized by drawing dog legs and ends up with a five-legged dog. So, the project begins to sour. Maybe the child decides dog-drawing is not her talent. She thinks of throwing the sketch away and going outside to play.

This is the place where parents and teachers can help by pointing out the commonness of problems for all artists. But they should use care in suggesting solutions, even if the way is obvious. The child creator may need the tension of searching and questioning in order to grow as an artist. Encouragement is the key here, a reminder that the solution is coming up.

5) The solution. Along with frustration comes incubation and then a solution, a moving forward. This can be a gradual realization or another aha! moment. Our girl artist may suddenly know that the fifth leg on the dog can be made to look like a tail. If the real pet has a stubby tail, perhaps this is, after all, a different dog. So begins the painting of a fantasy pet.

If a parent or teacher is around, here's a chance to rejoice along with the child, simply to marvel at the break-through. There are not too many places in a child-adult relationship where even ground exists. Usually the child is asking, declaring, pleasing and the adult is admonishing, advising, directing. Sharing a victory like this on equal ground with a parent or teacher can be extremely satisfying to a child.

Numbers 2 thru 5 are repeated numerous times, depending on the complexity of the project.

6) Now come the finishing touches, the completion of the work, the question of how to end the project. The dog's eyes blue or brown? Grass and flowers? Signing by the artist? Okay, it's show-and-tell and the painting is put up on the fridge. At this time, a new idea could be forming up from the original one. The seed has been sown. The dog painting has been so successful that the child begins thinking about a cat painting. So the sequence from 1) thru 6) may be repeated.

Creativity Involves Fluency, Originality, Flexibility, and Elaboration

These traits are often used in testing children for gifted-and-talented programs in schools. Think of them as partners with the foregoing steps in the creative process. When asked to give examples of these traits, Erren protested a bit: "For me, all of the categories are applicable in a big flurry when I am trying to 'be creative.' I suppose if I'm trying to solve a problem in a non-conventional way, I employ all these techniques, but when I try to parse them out...they all kind of seem the same."

Fluency suggests many ideas. Avrel's fluency takes the form of enlargement. "My intellectual life is driven by a compulsion to define, categorize, and through those surmise the biggest possible picture of the universe—always to 'zoom out,' in cinematic terms."

Originality is perhaps the most difficult of the creative virtues, since the common adage "there's nothing new under the sun" is so often quoted and believed. Still, originality suggests that a startling idea could be "brand new"—or at least so innovative that no one around can remember an historical use. "Re-imagining" or "re-tooling" may fit most of what we label original, though elements of our 20th and 21st century technology are broadly touted as utterly original. The iteration of primitive principles has been so remarkable that things which were labeled science fiction have come to be everyday reality.

Flexibility means the ability to change, to move outside the norm, to switch gears. In arranging furniture or mirrors or flowers, Erren says he might digress from the known use by asking himself, "Will this work upside down? Could I hang it on the wall or stack it? Does it make the room look bigger?"

Elaboration in creativity is the ability to add details, to flesh out whatever is brought forth, to recombine, or, as Avrel puts it, "to take it to the next step." He comments, "I've always felt this compulsion to do the next version of whatever it is that excites me at the moment...When

I finished *The Chronicles of Narnia* I geared up and wrote the eighth installment...When I read Ken Wilber's *The Marriage of Sense and Soul,* I decided to launch my own investigation of the cosmos and wrote *The Hull, The Sail, and the Rudder.*"

Ansen sees self-editing as a category of elaboration. "The idea of self-editing is something that has to be learned. As an adult artist, I feel that I'm constantly self-editing, not just on individual pieces of artwork, but even on a meta-scale, so that each new piece is improving on the last, expanding whatever visual or conceptual idea came before."

Skills and Competencies Bring
Creativity to Fruition

I once had a college student who was obsessed with his own creativity. He would bring me fifteen poems one day and fifteen new ones the next day, ones he had composed the night before. I barely had time to read the first batch before the next wave appeared. He was not concerned with skill-building, becoming a more competent poet—only with getting his work 'out there.' He did not want my honest assessment, only compliments.

After young artists have experienced some of the start-up qualities of creativity, like fluency and originality, they can be encouraged to pursue their chosen projects by practicing the skills of their discipline, in other words, settling down to perfect that flash of inspiration. The young composer with a fantastic tune or song in her head needs the discipline of learning to read music so she can notate her creations. The young dashing painter, filled with visions he wants to get on canvas, must spend time learning about surfaces, the thickness of paints, possible color combinations. There must be time and patience for application, testing, and struggle.

Nick Owen, an arts producer and researcher based in England, has studied how creativity in children can be killed and how it can be encouraged. "For some, the creative process is either the result of an unrestrained process of self expression and the unending generation of artifacts...or it is the result of a self-punishing process...of self-criticism and self-loathing, out of which is wrought their 'masterpiece.'...The process is more complex than either of these two positions suggests."[1]

Past the glamour and glory of their creations, older children need to be encouraged in apprenticeship, training, mastery.

About this, Ansen observed, "Probably like most young people, I believed that I'd be 'discovered' for some extraordinary talent. In reality, the 'discovery' by the outside world only comes from lots and lots of practice (and a little luck). Louis Pasteur said, 'Chance favors the prepared mind.' I believe this is true for creativity as well."

Character Strengths Buffer Creativity

About 25 years ago, I visited a fourth-grade classroom in an artist-in-education program designed to bring poets face to face with children in the public schools. When I entered the room that day, a boy on the front row slumped over his desk and uttered an "Awwwww" in what I perceived was a definite tone of disappointment.

Somewhat experienced by that time in these settings, I immediately set about to help him. "Hey, what's the matter?" I intoned in my best get-to-know-ya' voice.

He responded, "I thought a poet was a man, and that you would wear sandals and have scraggly toenails and a beard." I have cringed and laughed about that description many times since!

We have all known or heard of brilliant creative people whose talents went down in ashes because they did not have the character traits to sustain their creative passion. Perhaps they drank or did drugs, damaged their social relationships, or generally alienated themselves by their behavior both from others and from the wonderful potential of their talent.

Regardless of today's naysayers, some things do get better with time. One of those is the slow demise of the stereotypical image of the artist as a starving anti-social brilliant (male) misfit. In my own field of writing, I can think of many fine writers who keep regular writing hours, tend their families, and honor their social and civic responsibilities. They take baths, cut their toenails, and vote.

If children are to follow a lifelong commitment to their art, character strengths will be as important as artistic brilliance to sustain them through the inevitable ups and downs. They will need optimism, resilience, and persistence. The ability to delay rewards and to handle stress, to accept setbacks and analyze complexities will see them through rough patches. Conscientiousness and stamina will go a long way to satisfy their creative passions.

Joy Is the Ultimate Goal of Creativity

Sometimes the process is hard, the work arduous, but in the end we should all *feel better* for having entered into the creative process.

Past economic stability, competition, recognition, or family tradition is finding one's bliss in art-making. Avrel's comment on childhood art, "We all just did whatever was fun for us" encapsulates this ultimate rationale.

Albert Einstein gave a challenge to parents and teachers. "It is the supreme art of the teacher to awaken joy in creative expression and knowledge."[1]

There is nothing quite like the high of being "in flow." Time passes without notice. Life goes on around. The passion of creation takes center stage. The fun of it buoys one along.

The sons' statements on this mysterious lift bear repeating:

Ansen sees joy in "the process of producing the art...always different, always changing."

Erren describes "that soul-filling feeling that you get when creativity is really flowing. Sometimes you get it gardening, or painting, or decorating for Christmas. It's that pure fun feeling when you're making something out of nothing. It's just coming out of you with no resistance."

Avrel's take on this ineffable emotion rising up from creating: "When a person is fulfilling a true calling, the soul stirs and moves in ways that I only know how to describe as fulfillment—the sensation that you are doing that which you have been put on the earth to do."

Catching the brightness, the soulfulness, the sheer happiness of making art is of inestimable value to any human. For the child, it may be enough to inform a lifetime.

Creating is finding the sweet spot.

Part Seven: Final Thoughts

Final Thoughts

Finally, as Saint Paul was wont to write when he was almost finished for the third time with one of his epistles, I want to say briefly here what doesn't fit into other parts of this book.

Clarissa Estés, in her book *Women Who Run With the Wolves*, writes, "I'm not certain how many friends one needs, but definitely one or two who think your gift, whatever it may be, is *pan de cielo*, the bread of heaven."[1]

We had a world-class family friend named Bob Sherman. He hung out with us, asked questions about our work and lives, stayed with our children while we took trips, landscaped our yard, and wrote us treasured letters. Bob would manage to attend an opera or ballet written by Carl and say afterward, "I just don't see how you did that!"

He would listen with serious attention while eleven-year-old Avrel told him a long fantastical tale. Bob would ask me to read one of my poems to him. Bob's loving curious presence for thirty years in our lives made a huge difference. It's not possible to order up a friend like Bob, but if you should locate the likes of him, recognize the treasure that such a person is, to the world and to your family.

Here I'd also like to put in a word for family cohesion. An article in the *Journal of Secondary Gifted Education* discusses what kinds of families promote creativity that is apt to continue when the children become adults. Surprisingly enough, creative children brought up in calm reliable affluent families did not necessarily show an outstanding tendency to become creative adults. Of course there are notable exceptions, but in the study it was those children in families with some disorder, some push-back or hardship whose children carried their creativity forward into adulthood.[2]

I have written earlier about our periods of genteel poverty. I think this fact may have had a great deal to do with instilling in our children traits of emotional intelligence which carried through to their adult lives. With our closely monitored finances and extreme frugality there was a discipline of wants and material desires. Free play, time alone, and being different from their more affluent friends built character, work habits, stamina, and boldness.

In a study of Chinese children selected for their creativity for higher education, it was found "that family cohesion...conceptualized as the family's encouragement of members' conformity and interdependence, rather than independence, did not impede creativity, but instead significantly predicted creativity."[3] The Seales are a long way from the culture of Chinese families. How valid is this principle for us? To a degree I think it is true.

Connectivity, not only with each other in our immediate family but also and especially how we find our niche generationally, has been of importance in our family.

Our boys were fortunate to have had a great extended family with whom we interacted frequently. They knew all four grandparents, with fondness going both ways. Carl's father made wooden toys for them in his shop and took them fishing. My father taught all three to drive. How can we ever thank him!

Both grandmothers were warm, active people who thought up ways to engage them. Carl's mother made handmade Christmas presents for them—appliquéd shirts and individual quilts. My mother encouraged their playing on her organ and interested them in plants she grew. Each set of grandparents served dutifully through summer weeks as child-keepers. The boys had three sets of aunts and uncles. They have eleven cousins.

An incident Ansen reported illustrates connectivity. Ansen was given Carl's father's lathe from his woodworking shop. Not being sure of all its properties, Ansen went to the San Antonio public library and discovered a manual for this particular tool. On it was stamped "Trinity Library, Waxahachie." Trinity University in San Antonio, his alma mater, was first located in Waxahachie, the little central Texas town where I graduated from high school and where Ansen's maternal grandparents lived in retirement. A dizzy set of coincidences. Ansen reported that in this discovery he felt an almost magical connection with the world. Both sets of grandparents, his own education, an adult curiosity—the Universe was surely looking out for him.

Lastly, I would say that respect for the child and his creative endeavor was key to our sons' permanent creativity in the arts. If we did anything right, I think it was our parental mantra, early on: Let them do whatever they want to, as long as they don't hurt themselves or others. This must be what prompted Ansen to observe: "I think that is what defines our family, that we have such energy and lack of fear in our endeavors."

Carl and I were abiding by our own house rule. In us were reflected the craziness, the impracticality, the deep longing and the irrational passion of art. The sons felt the yearning and the highs and lows. They knew for themselves the love of bringing something new into the light. It was their nature, their nurture, and something else, quite indefinable, the uniqueness of each of their individual selves.

Appendix

Ansen: A Montage

Fall, 1979

First letter home after going to college:

Things are going great guns up here! I'm usually so busy I can hardly keep up. The two jobs take up most of my free time and I'm enjoying both. My classes are all good and I'm happy for really good profs. The most enjoyable class is probably my photo critique conference with Bill Bristow. He is such an intelligent and visually aware person that I think he'll be a long-lasting friend (but not for only those reasons).

Guess what? I'm developing a style! Yeah!..I finally feel like I'm growing now.

1986 –an essay

There's a silver metal line crossing the asphalt road in the middle of Falcon Dam in the Rio Grande Valley of Texas. It divides the United States from Mexico. When I was young, my family went on outings to the lake formed by that dam and whenever I could slip away, I walked out to the middle of the dam.

I looked down at the tremendous drop to the water and up at the buzzards spiraling on the thermals created by the huge concrete structure. Very few cars travelled that road then, so I stood on one side of the silver line and then the other, trying in twelve-year-old logic to discern any subtle difference in the way I felt. Being in another country should make you "feel" different, right?

The line itself was about six inches wide, broad enough for a careful boy to place his feet heel to toe and walk the breadth of the roadway. When I did this, I assumed I was in No-Man's Land. What a concept! Little did I know, looking up at the birds circling unconcerned in their international air, that I would come to see in this

167

unique place a metaphor for the life work I would choose.

When I was 17, I bought a used Pentax and proclaimed myself a photographer. The interest stuck like no other hobby I had ever tried. Technology and art: they held my interest on both sides.

A lot of water passed through the dam and I found myself graduating from Trinity University with a degree in Communications and Studio Art, with an emphasis on photography. But not without a certain amount of guilt...

I felt a keen sense of guilt banging out pictures in the darkroom overnight while my art professor and mentor labored weeks and months over each painting....

If I may wax Freudian for a moment, some photographers never seem to get over this guilt and end up desperately trying to impose themselves on their pictures. All artists, to some degree, have to be a little egotistical, and the stereotype of artist looking down his nose at artisan and technician is enduring and not totally baseless. But the fact that photography records so well and yet so meaningfully pushes the artist/photographer right into the middle. He's caught between unbridled paint-slinging creativity on one hand and a demand for highly technical skills on the other.

In the spectrum of artists/photographers, at one end we have the techno-nerd who can draw you the notch code of every sheet film made since l946. At the other extreme is the groovy art school grad who thinks dust spots should be left alone, "like, they're part of the process, man."

So I, as do most photographers, find myself in No-Man's Land. I must walk the silver stripe, but carefully. I have my share of ego and the desire for my personality to show in my work. The projects I've taken on lately though call for real restraint in this area. I've come to know some of the virtues of having a transparent personality, of being the medium and not the message in my work.

1989--Here Ansen is commenting on having been the photographer for an archeological dig in Tuscany, and home again, being hired to photograph the prison art on the walls of the old Bexar County jail before it was demolished.

In my own artwork this idea of being the silent recorder, the transparent personality, has taken on a life of its own. What stands in front of the camera does all the talking. I hardly ever rearrange things to take a shot. Instead, I arrange my own vantage point, lens, film, etc. to take advantage of what already exists. I'm out to reveal the interesting things I see around me. Reality is stranger than fiction—and to me, more interesting. The viewer is caught off guard by the vantage point or the strange situation but, at the same time, can't deny that this is reality. Photographs are surreal.

Photographers who call themselves artistic "walk the line" between art and purely functional illustration. I enjoy the ambiguity of that situation. It gives me the freedom to choose what I want to be at any moment, artist or technician. Being a photographer is like having two passports.

Fall, 2001—[from an article in the Trinity alumni magazine by Mary Denny]

We see photographs as proxies of reality, but they are not reality any more than a map is a real landscape. Therein lies the power of photography, to be a representation of reality...An artist is always trying to project his own internal reality to the world.

About slitscan photography—2006 [from an article in *San Antonio Magazine*, Dec.-Jan. 2006 by Jon Gillespie]

The panoramic camera I invented is ideal for doing a virtual tour and that was its original purpose. But now I'm subverting its purpose to make art.
. . . .
My work has always split the difference between photography and painting. I wanted my photography to be much more about the medium than the subject. There's a reality that we're not privileged to see. We can only view it through this camera.

On his series "Bloodlines" in which he used his own blood as the printing medium [from an online article in *Fogged Clarity – An Arts Review*, 2009, by Andy Douglas]

Blood has a very sturdy chemical composition. There's such permanence in it. I was interested in blood's positive aspects. It carries all this info – who you are, what you ate for breakfast, what your emotions are. I wanted to extend my emotions in this way onto the print. My blood is something uniquely mine. Using it as material also creates a kind of visual exclamation point – to say 'I mean this!'

. . . .

Numbers, to me, are as interesting as art as they are as mathematics. A friend had a dream in which prime numbers were chasing him down the street. Fantastic! It awoke something in me. What if numbers are real, I thought, what if they have personalities? What if they exist outside our perception of them? I'm taking a layman's understanding of mathematics, and putting it into a different context, that of art.

From an article in the *San Antonio Express-News*, Sept. 24, 2010 by Steve Bennett

I have found slitscan photography to be an excellent vehicle for ideas central to my work—ideas about time and our place in its continuum. Instead of mirroring the world as we know it, I believe this camera records a hidden reality...A single sliver of space is imaged over an extended period of time, yielding the surprising result that unmoving objects are blurred and moving bodies are rendered clearly...I tease out this unusual reality lurking just beneath the surface of our everyday visual experience in the same way cubist painters created dynamic tension by exploiting the interplay between what the viewer expects and what she gets.

Erren: A Montage

From an article in *McNews*, 2010 by Roda Grubb

People should live artfully and be surrounded by quality things because that will improve their living. If your place is happy, your surroundings are happy—your house, your office—then you'll enjoy life more. It helps make you more calm and appreciative of life.

From an article in *The Monitor*, November 2009

"Tribute to a Tree"
This beautiful old Date Palm had been blown sideways by Hurricane Beulah in 1967, but had started to grow upright again by 1972. It was in the yard of an old farm house my family had rented north of McAllen. We played on it, climbed on it, and chased our dog Taffy up and down its bumpy trunk...It's important because in a flat place like the Valley, trees are the only things we have to look up at.

From *The Mesquite Review*, 1999

"Searching for a South Texas Style in Home Décor"
There is a decorating revolution on the horizon. The long-obedient South Texas home owner is about to rise up against convention and beat back the advances of mauve carpeting and country goose-covered wallpaper. Now is the time to be courageous, to think creatively, and to invent a new style for South Texas living.

There's really nothing new under the sun in the world of decorating. Ever since the first cave woman decided to throw saber-tooth tiger pillows around the campfire, we've been stealing the best ideas from previous generations to incorporate into our own home—keeping what we like, throwing out the impractical, and dabbling in current trends to keep ourselves amused. The trick to effective decorating is balancing drama, comfort and 'resonance.'

Resonance is the ring of truth that a decorating style has—how it fits with the architecture, culture and history of an area. It's what makes a room feel like a real place and not a movie set or an imitation of magazine pages.

One of the decorating 'styles' of the moment (at least in our area) seems to be Southwest. At Southwest's epicenter is Santa Fe, New Mexico, where you'll find great examples of old adobe buildings adorned with worn wooden doors and high rows of round vigas sticking out of clay-colored walls. Interiors might feature a mix of Native American textiles and ceramics blended with the muted palette of the desert, as well as elements of Spanish colonial influence. When done well, Santa Fe Style represents an elegant reflection of the quiet passage of centuries. At its worst, it's a cliché of turquoise coyotes and garish knock-offs of Navaho designs. The main problem with whole-hog transplantation of Southwest style to South Texas is that most of its main elements don't resonate with our area. Without any cultural reference, those blanket-wrapped Native Americans and pink saguaro cactus pillows look as foreign in the Valley as mountains and pine trees.

So where's our connection? Head south. Since our land, and much of our Valley culture, came from Mexico, that seems a good place to start. Mexico has a wealth of decorating ideas and styles that Valleyites can adopt with ease.

Today's Mexican artisans have borrowed heavily from the visual vocabulary of the Catholic baroque churches, deep relief altars swimming with highly carved angels, columns, shells and swirls in gold leaf, saintly statues, gleaming brass candlesticks, richly colored oil paintings and yards of hanging velvet.

Using centuries-old themes like Our Lady of Guadalupe and the symbolic sacred heart, they have created a mind-boggling array of crosses, nichos, shelves and furniture. The good news is if you like this style, more is always better. Layer it on. Add church candles, incense and flowers and you'll have your own personal sacred space. Whether the imagery has religious significance to you, or you just like the Old World look, you'll enjoy rearranging wall space and table tops to see if you can fit in 'just one more piece.'

Mexican Country Style has also emerged as a popular trend in home décor. This style features the rustic furniture used in everyday

life by the common people of Mexico (and our border in the early 20th
century). Old tables and benches from ranchos and markets, worn lovingly by time and chipped in all the right places, can now live proudly beside the finest antiques in your home.

The more creative you are the better. An old 'V' shaped feed trough set on end can be made into a terrific corner cabinet. An ox yolk swinging in an arch out on the patio adds loads of charm, with or without planted baskets of purslane hanging from each end. Or set out piloncillos (antique sugar molds from Veracruz), long boards with rows of cone-shaped holes carved in them, which are ready for dried flowers or candles.

An old trastero (kitchen hutch) filled with Guadalajara tourist pottery from the 30s and 40s instantly transports you to abuelita's kitchen (even if your grandmother is a gringa like mine). Or hang an antique sombrero (a real one—not the sequined border variety) on the wall to add the visual interest of a great piece of art at a fraction of the price.

Now, take a big wooden spoon and stir all these styles up. Add a few Valley icons like potted palms or a bowl of fresh yellow limes, perhaps a nostalgic Valley landscape oil by Gabriel Salazar, and plenty of old family photos. Be brave with color. Do a little research, then go wild with your wall paint: deep rich colors always make your furnishings stand out. Don't be afraid to mix the fancy with the rustic. Your interior should be an intuitive eclectic mix of the things you like.

Presto! You've created South Texas Style. Now go make a pitcher of margaritas, plop down in a comfy chair and toast your creativity.

Avrel: How We Made an Epic Film
for Less than $1,000

In an era when a "low-budget" film is often considered to be something made for about $1 million, I think my friend Jay Galvan and I may have recalibrated things a bit. In 2005, we made a feature-length movie called The Secret of Suranesh for less than $1,000. In the fall of 2004, Jay told me he had just bought a new digital video camera that rendered video that looked like film. Having gotten a degree in radio-TV-film in the late eighties, I was well-versed in the difference between the look of video and the look of film, so I was skeptical, but not having worked in the field, I was largely ignorant of the huge advances that had occurred in the intervening 15 years. All the same, I was curious.

The next time we met, he brought his laptop and showed me five minutes' worth of test footage he had shot in his backyard on his Canon XL2. I was in.

Over the next few months we toyed with what we might do with this new ability. At first we considered making a short, or a series of shorts. Then we thought about undertaking a documentary, the only option that seemed rational for two guys with virtually no budget.

But as we continued brainstorming we eventually talked each other into jumping off the deep-end with a full-length feature film. One thing remained the same, though: we had virtually no money.

Jay had some pictures in his head, as did I. Both of us saw a sort of lonely, post-apocalyptic world, which fit nicely with our budget for sets: $0. But futuristic apocalypses had become pretty cliché. I kept thinking of the Planet of the Apes, The Terminator, and Mad Max.

What had not been done, that I was aware of, was the portrayal of a post-apocalyptic world set in the past. This concept played right into a long-held interest of mine in lost civilizations, one influenced heavily by the writings of Graham Hancock (Fingerprints of the Gods, Underworld).

175

As I got busy writing the script, Jay got busy investigating every setting on the camera, to see how far we could push it toward a film look — lots of talk of color saturation, grain, and how black we could get the blacks.

Knowing that we were going to actually make this movie informed every aspect of the script. No large armies. No exotic animals. In fact, the entire cast was six people, plus two others with brief non-speaking roles. No lavish costumes. Jay and I spent about $300 on leather and fabric and fashioned all the costumes ourselves, even recycling different pieces of cloth in different configurations for different characters. I did the makeup, even learning how to lay a crepe-wool beard. All of the props came either out of my garage or from Goodwill.

After we had settled on our premise, the chief concern while shooting became avoiding any and all signs of modernity. To accomplish this, we shot in city, county, state, and national parks, most within an hour's drive of Austin. On one three-day weekend, site unseen except from snapshots on the Web, we took our lead character, "Suranesh," played by a really good-natured and patient friend named Joe Fradella, and made the drive to West Texas to run him around Big Bend National Park and Monahans Sandhills State Park (3,000 acres of sand dunes that provided our archetypal desert). Those three days of shooting gave the film virtually all of its "epic" scale, because we interspersed those "traveling" shots between scenes of dialogue that were filmed relatively tight. I think the effect worked pretty well. On another three-day weekend, we took Suranesh down to the Rio Grande Valley to shoot the last fourth of the movie in a tropical setting, including the coast.

In nearly every shot of the movie, some sign of modernity is just out of frame, be it a trash can on Boca Chica Beach, a handrail at Hamilton Pool, a fire hydrant in the middle of a creek, an oil rig just over the horizon of a Monahans dune, or the ubiquitous cigarette butts and jet trails. But I've watched every scene in the movie about 100 times now and haven't spotted any slip-ups on that front. The hard part in post-production was getting the sound clean, as the microphone was picking up 18-wheelers and barking dogs a mile away when we didn't even hear them on set.

All of the cast and crew were volunteers. Having all non-actors as actors did create a directing challenge, but we got by with a cue card system that worked pretty well in most cases, so that our friends did not have to memorize lines. And the crew was lean, to say the least. The standard config was Jay behind the camera, one person holding the boom mic, and me supervising the script and holding cue cards. It was a luxury when we had a fourth person, who could hold the bounce card to fill shadows, or help wrangle props or unruly costumes or hair, or just listen and watch for continuity.

Not only was it lean on set, but it was quick. Jay and I both have full-time jobs and young children, so we had to optimize our time away from home. Plus, all of our talent was volunteer and we didn't want to take advantage of our friends' time and good will. So one element that was crucial to our success was knowing what we wanted, sticking to the script, being organized, and not fooling around a lot on set. We had to get out there, get the shot, and get back home to the wife, kids, and job. We did relatively few retakes, and we wound up using just about every shot we got. Not much margin for error.

We shot the movie in 12 days over the course of five weeks. About six months after principal photography, we realized we needed some more B-roll, so we took a day trip down to a Renaissance festival, where we shot a lot of quirky, non-identifiable footage that we were able to roll in. We also shot footage on my uncle's horse ranch, and found a skyscraper in downtown Houston the top of which resembles a Mayan temple. No need to build a model — we just shot it from the ground, cropping it above the air conditioning units. (We did have to clone out the little red blinking air-traffic control light on top.)

Low-budget film making is like a scavenger hunt. If your script calls for something, you just keep your eyes open until you see it. Since it was almost all shot in nature, we took what we got. If it was cloudy on a particular day, it was cloudy in the movie. If it was a spectacular sunset, we got a spectacular sunset. Again, little to no margin for retakes. In that sense, it felt a little like God had a hand in the look of the film. The weather was what it was, but time and again, we got exactly what we needed. The sun would break through right when we needed it, the clouds, when we needed them.

Editing took about six months, and was all on Jay's laptop. If we had had 40 hours a week to devote to it, we probably could have knocked it out in about a month, but we did it by hook or crook, collaborating over dozens of lunch hours and the occasional all-nighter to get it done.

The last major piece, the music, which is equally important as the cinematography in giving it an epic feel, happened by sheer accident of birth. It just so happens that my father, Carl Seale, is a lifelong composer in the symphonic idiom that the film needed, and, since the 1990s, has become accomplished in digital orchestration. He composed the soundtrack and recorded all of the orchestration, basically just for fun. (He also acted in the movie.) So I highly recommend having extremely talented family members when you're making an epic for no money.

All in all, I think we pulled it off. We spent 2006 entering it in film festivals to no avail. But we took it straight to DVD in late 2006, through on-demand fulfillment, and viewer reaction has been heartwarming. We've sold copies in 19 states, plus Canada, the U.K., Germany, New Zealand, and South Africa. One viewer has listed it in her top-10 movies of all time. Can't ask for much more than that!

And we did it all for less than $1,000, most of which was gasoline and breakfast tacos for our cast and crew. (If you're starting with absolutely nothing, the camera, computer, and software probably would run about $5,000, maybe less today.) It's been an adventure.

Notes

Introduction
  1. *Time,* June 11, 1990, 40.
  2. Andrew Newberg, *How God Changes Your Brain,* 166.
  3. E.M. Forster, *Aspects of the Novel,* Chapter Five: The Plot.
  4. Martin Winchester, e-mail, Jan. 27, 2005.
  5. David Shenk, *The Genius in All of Us, 77.*

Part One: Beginnings
  Another Seale Pup: Avrel
    1. Jan Seale, *Sharing the House,* 20.

Part Three: Presently
  Ansen: Art and commercial photography
    1. Seale, 32.
    2. Jennifer James, *Defending Yourself Against Criticism,* 26.
    3. *Time,* June 11, 1990, 52.
  Erren: Graphic design and cultural arts
    1. Seale, 21.
  Avrel: Writing and music
    1. Avrel Seale, *True Freedom,* 96-7.
    2. Daniel Coyle, *The Talent Code,* 14.
  Carl: Musical passion and mission
    1. http://www.goodreads.com/quotes
  Jan: Writing and teaching
    1. Jan Seale, *Airlift: Short Stories.*
    2. Robert Louis Stevenson, *A Child's Garden of Verses,* xxiv "Happy Thought."

Part Four: The Home as Lab
  Free Time and the Make-it Drawer
    1. *Child of Our Time: Killing Creativity,*
       www.open2.net/childofourtime/2007/creativity.
  Encouragement
    1. Avrel Seale, *True Freedom,* 94.
  Training
    1. Geoff Colvin, *Talent is Overrated,* 23.
    2. Madeleine L'Engle, http://www.brainyquote.com
  Discipline
    1. Elaine Aron, *The Highly Sensitive Person.*
    2. Sharon Heller, *Too Loud, Too Bright, Too Fast, Too Tight.*
  Television
    1. Avrel Seale, *Dude,* 41-56.
    2. Ellen Handler Spitz, *The Brightening Glance: Imagination and Childhood,* 227.
  Collaborations
    1. Anne Bernays and Justin Kaplan, "Can This Collaboration Be Saved?" *The New York Times Book Review,* n.d., 31.

Part Five: Considerations
  Genes
    1. Michael Rutter as quoted in *The Genius in All of Us,* 93.
    2. Shenk, 135-6.
    3. *The Week,* Jan. 25, 2013, 9.
  Sensitivity
    1. Aron, 7.
  Personalities
    1. Susan Cain, *Quiet: The Power of Introverts in a World That Can't Stop Talking.* Chapter 1.
    2. quoted in Cain, 14.
  Humors and Muses
    1. "Daily OM." "Compelled to Create." June 21, 2007, www.dailyom.com.

Part Six: Cultivating Creativity
   Creativity in family life
        1. Spitz, 5.
   Hardship
        1. Jan Seale, "Art in the Boonies," *riverSedge*, vol. 1,
          no. 3, 36.
        2. Tim Gill, "We Don't Need No Supervision," *Ode,*
          January/February 2008, 32.

   High IQ and good grades
        1. Albert Einstein: www.brainyquote.com/quotes/
          quotes/a/alberteins.
        2. Paul Tough, *How Children Succeed, 48.*
   Skills
        1. Nick Owen, www.open2.net/childofourtime/2007/
          creativity.html.
   Joy
        1. Einstein: www.brainyquote.com./quotes/quotes/
          a/alberteins.

Part Seven*:* Final Thoughts
   Final Thoughts
        1. Clarissa Pinkola Estés, *Women Who Run With the*
          Wolves, p. 348.
        2. "Self-perceived creativity, family hardiness,
          and emotional intelligence..." *Journal of Secondary*
          Gifted Education, March 22, 2005. Online.
        3. Ibid.

Works Consulted

Aron, Elaine N. *The Highly Sensitive Person: How to Thrive When the World Overwhelms You*. Secaucus, N.J.: A Birch Lane Press Book, published by Carol Publishing Group, 1996.

Bernays, Anne and Justin Kaplan. "Can This Collaboration Be Saved?" *The New York Times Book Review*, n.d.

Berry, Thomas. *Evening Thoughts: Reflecting on Earth as Sacred Community*. San Francisco: Sierra Club Books, 2006.

Cain, Susan. *Quiet: The Power of Introverts in a World That Can't Stop Talking*. New York: Broadway Paperbacks, 2013.

Campbell, Joseph. http://www.goodreads.com/quotes.

Cocks, Jay. "Let's Get Crazy." *Time*, June 11, 1990:40-1.

Colvin, Geoff. *Talent is Overrated*. New York: Portfolio Trade, 2010.

"Compelled to Create." "Daily OM." [blog] June 21, 2007.

Coyle, Daniel. *The Talent Code*. New York: Bantam Dell (Random House), 2009.

Einstein, Albert. www.brainyquote.com/quotes.

Estés, Clarissa Pinkola. *Women Who Run With the Wolves*. New York: Ballantine Books, 1992.

Fritz, Jennifer. "State of the Arts" interview. *The Monitor*, Aug. 26, 1990.

Gill, Tim. "We Don't Need No Supervision," *Ode,* January/February 2008:32.

Hart, Tobin. *The Secret Spiritual World of Children*. Novato, California: New World Library, 2003.

Heller, Sharon. *Too Loud, Too Bright, Too Fast, Too Tight*. New York: *HarperCollins, 2002*.

James, Jennifer. *Defending Yourself Against Criticism*. Middlebury, Vermont: Newmarket Press, 1993.

Jaroff, Leon. "He Gives Wings to Dreams." *Time,* June 11,1990: 52+.

Owen, Nick, producer. "Killing Creativity," http://www.open2.net/childofourtime/2007/creativity.html

Lawlis, Frank. *The IQ Answer*. New York: Viking, 2006.

L'Engle, Madeleine. www.brainyquote.com

Newberg, Andrew. *How God Changes Your Brain*. New York: Ballantine Books, 2010.

Schirrmacher, Robert. *Art and Creative Development for Young Children*. Third edition. Albany, New York: Delmar Publishers, 1998.

Seale, Avrel. *Dude*. Privately published, 2008.

_____. *True Freedom*. Privately published, 2007.

Seale, Jan. *Airlift: Short Stories*. Ft. Worth, Texas: TCU Press, 1992.

_____. "Art in the Boonies." *riverSedge*, vol. 1, no. 3: 36.

_____. *Homeland: Essays Beside and Beyond the Rio Grande*. Edinburg, Texas: New Santander Press, 1995.

_____. *Sharing the House*. riverSedge Press Poetry Series. Edinburg, Texas,1982.

"Self-perceived creativity, family hardiness, and emotional intelligence..." *Journal of Secondary Gifted Education,* March 22, 2005.

Shenk, David. *The Genius in All of Us: Why Everything You've Been Told About Genetics, Talent, and IQ Is Wrong*. New York: Doubleday, 2010.

Spitz, Ellen Handler. *The Brightening Glance: Imagination and Childhood*. New York: Pantheon Books, 2006.

Stevenson, Robert Louis. *A Child's Garden of Verses*. United Kingdom: Echo Library, 2005.

"The 'switches' on your genes." *The Week*, Jan. 25, 2013:9.

The Town Crier, McAllen, Texas.

Tough, Paul. *How Children Succeed: Grit, Curiosity, and the Hidden Power of Character*. Boston, Massachusetts: Houghton Mifflin Harcourt, 2012.

Other books from Angelina River Press

Memoirs
> *Adventures from the Last Century*, Carl Craven
> *Memoirs of a Biologist*, Gail Fail

Novel
> *The Wild Part*, Jerry Craven

Short Fiction and Essays
> *Field Guide*, Steve Sherwood

For information on these and other books go to
www.angelinariverpress.com

Jan Seale, the 2012 Texas Poet Laureate, is a native Texan living on the Texas-Mexico border. Her writing includes books of poetry, essays, and short fiction. She has three sons and four grandsons. Her husband Carl died in 2014.

www.janseale.com

www.ingramcontent.com/pod-product-compliance
Lightning Source LLC
Chambersburg PA
CBHW031131090426
42738CB00008B/1051